MW00611516

A Winding Road:
A Handbook for those Supporting the Suicide Bereaved

Michelle Linn-Gust, Ph.D. & John Peters, M.Suicidology

A Winding Road: A Handbook for those Supporting the Suicide Bereaved

ISBN: 978-09723318-2-1

Library of Congress Control Number: 2010913533

Chellehead Works books are available at special discounts when purchased in bulk for premiums and sales promotions as well as fundraising and educational use.

For details, contact the Special Sales Director at:

info@chelleheadworks.com
505-266-3134 (voice)
Albuquerque, New Mexico
www.chelleheadworks.com

Printed in the United Kingdom

First printing October 2010

Book Cover Photo of Bryn y Gwynt, North Wales by Pierino Algieri
www.algieri-images.co.uk

Book cover design by Giselle Burns (http://www.giselles.co.uk)

Layout designed by Megan Herndon

Distribution in Europe • Argoed Books – john@johnpeters.freeserve.co.uk

~ Meet the Co-Authors ~

MICHELLE LINN-GUST, Ph.D.

Michelle Linn-Gust is an international author and speaker about suicide prevention and postvention issues as well as the importance of dog companionship, particularly after loss. She is the author of *Rocky Roads: The Journeys of Families through Suicide Grief* and *Ginger's Gift: Hope and Healing Through Dog Companionship*. Her first book, based on the suicide of her younger sister Denise, *Do They Have Bad Days in Heaven? Surviving the Suicide Loss of a Sibling*, inspired siblings around the world in their survival after a loved one's suicide. She is the President-Elect for the American Association of Suicidology. She lives in Albuquerque, New Mexico, in the U.S.A. Read more about Michelle at www.michellelinngust.com.

JOHN PETERS, M.SUICIDOLOGY

John Peters originates from North Wales and originally trained in Agriculture. He worked in Kenya with the Ministry of Agriculture for ten years before returning to the U.K. to train as a teacher and achieved a degree in psychology. He lost his son, Dale, to suicide eighteen years ago and has since devoted an increasing amount of time to supporting others who have been bereaved by suicide, principally with the U.K. charity Survivors of Bereavement by Suicide. His studies of the subject have led to a Masters in Suicidology from Griffith University. He is a member of the International Association of Suicide Prevention and an active member of its Postvention Task Force. John regularly conducts training sessions for professionals and others in the understanding of suicide bereavement and is a regular guest tutor at Coventry University. His main additional interest is singing with the Canoldir Male Choir, also acting as its secretary.

~ Guest Author Bios ~

Pam Dean, M.Ed. Counselling, MBACP, lives in Derbyshire, U.K., and became a survivor in 1999 when her first husband ended his life. She has worked with survivors in group settings and in individual therapy. Having worked with primary school children, Pam has become particularly interested in the use of art, in its many forms, when working with young people. Pam qualified as a counsellor in 1996, gaining her Masters in 1998.

Emily Duval, M.A., Psychology, MBACP, Accred., was born in California and became a survivor when her boyfriend died by suicide in 1993. Having lost two extended family members to suicide, she also has particular empathy for families. Emily has been working with survivors in both group and individual therapy settings since 1998. She earned her degrees in San Francisco and immigrated to the United Kingdom in 2004 and currently works as a psychotherapist in London.

Jill Fisher, M.Suicidology, is the National Coordinator for the StandBy Response Service based at United Synergies Ltd. on Australia's Sunshine Coast which she was instrumental in setting up. She now oversees the implementation of StandBy across several Australian sites. StandBy is a community-based active postvention programme, providing a 24-hour integrated response to suicide bereavement. Jill is an active member on several national and international committees and is the current editor of the IASP Postvention Task Force Newsletter.

Michelle Flood, D.Ed Psych, is from Co Leitrim, Ireland. Michelle's early experience of bereavement, when her brother died from SIDS in 1988 when she was six years old, influenced her decision to pursue a career in Child Psychology. She has recently completed her Doctorate in Educational, Child, and Adolescent Psychology in Queen's University Belfast. For her doctoral thesis, Michelle investigated the impact of bereavement by suicide on the family unit and hopes to continue her career in this area.

Mark Haith, MA, qualified as a mental health nurse in 2003 and as a counsellor in 2004. He began working with people with mental health problems in 1997 and is a specialist in the field of CBT. He has been successful in helping clients with emotional difficulties, mental health problems, behavioural issues, drug and alcohol use, eating disorders, obsessional traits and self-harming behaviours. Mark currently teaches mental health at Robert Gordon University, Aberdeen, U.K.

"Mary" (name changed) is from Northen Ireland. She lost her partner to suicide after being together for eight years. She contacted the Helpline of Survivors of Bereavement by Suicide (U.K.) and her contribution shows the help that can be obtained through a self-support organisation. "Mary's Story" illustrates the change in a person's life after a suicide and gives much hope to those who have been recently bereaved.

Tracy McLeod was brought up in Hawick, Scotland. Her son, Mark, was born when she was seventeen and her parents agreed to bring up Mark but Tracy was always Mum. Mark was bullied at school and took his own life at the age of twenty. Tracy became a regular member of a self-support group and this contribution is in the form of a conversation between Tracy and Mark which she eloquently delivered at the Birmingham U.K. Support Day in May 2010.

Rick Mogil, the Program Director of the Suicide Prevention and Bereavement Services at the Didi Hirsch Mental Health Services in Los Angeles, California, lost his younger brother to suicide in 2003. He initially participated in a bereavement support group through the organization's Survivor After Suicide Program before becoming a volunteer, co-facilitator, writer for the newsletter, and a member of the suicide response team before joining the paid staff.

TABLE OF CONTENTS

~ Preface ~

WHY THE SURVIVORS' PERSPECTIVE

For John this scene represents the start of his Winding Road for is was here in the idyllic countryside of North Wales that he was told by the police of the death of his son whilst staying at his daughter's house

This book is intended to provide support for any who are helping those bereaved by suicide. We hope that this will be an accessible book that can assist a variety of professionals, volunteers, and friends who, in their different ways, may find themselves in a situation that they need to be of help to a bereaved survivor. With rates of 11.1 per 100,00 in the USA and 6.8 per 100,000 in the UK suicide is not as common a form of death as others. This has meant that the subject of suicide bereavement has been given a very low profile in most training courses for those who might have to cope with the effects of suicide. However for the one who is bereaved by suicide the rate appears to be 100%. We consider that there is still much stigma attached to suicide and this adds to the difficulty in preparation for the possibility of dealing with suicide bereavement.

Both principal authors (and a number of the guest authors) have themselves been bereaved by suicide, both have furthered their academic knowledge of the subject by advanced study, and both continue to work on a regular basis with survivors. Most importantly, we share a passion to improve the support afforded to those bereaved by suicide.

It is from this combination of personal experience, detailed study, and, most importantly, the knowledge gleaned from fellow survivors that continue to inform the authors. It is hoped that this experience can be used to help any person who has been bereaved by suicide.

We start by stressing the importance of the need to use appropriately sensitive language, so essential when helping the suicide bereaved, and then we look at the factors that have influenced the way that society views suicide and particularly how it views suicide bereavement.

The effect that suicide has on the family, children, and adolescents is addressed with contributions based on research carried out by Michelle Linn-Gust and Michelle Flood, followed by Emily Duval's description of her experiences in dealing with suicide in the workplace.

We then look at ways that the suicide bereaved can be supported with descriptions of the value of practical help from telephone and group support. This support is underlined by two personal descriptions of the road of recovery by Tracy and Mary followed by an account of the research by Michelle Flood into the behavior and practice of others, including professionals, on the bereavement experience.

A variety of bereavement support practices are then described including a description of the StandBy project in Australia by Jill Fisher, the use of art therapy in England by Pam Dean, the pioneering work of the Didi Hirsch Center in the United States, and the role of pet animals in bereavement, again, in the United States.

We conclude with a fascinating description of the way that the death by suicide affected a young professional by Mark Haith and by examining how professionals and others can support those who have been bereaved by suicide.

We hope that this combination of experience, theory, and practice will help the reader to better understand the feelings of the suicide bereaved when they are called upon to help survivors by having more confidence in their task.

~ John Peters
September 2010

~ Foreword ~

To metaphorically speak to what the publisher probably will not choose to print, "S____ happens." In this case, read that as "Suicide happens." Suicides happen more than 34,000 times a year in the United States and an estimated 900,000 times a year across the globe. Nobody, but nobody seeks to be a survivor of suicide. Survivorship is thrust upon those who loved, lived with, worked with, went to school with, and otherwise knew well enough to be impacted by the individual who died by suicide. And when we count the numbers of those who tell us they were significantly and emotionally impacted by a death by suicide, it is easy to understand that suicides have a deep and lasting effect on our society. This is just one more in a long list of reasons why we should do everything possible to prevent suicide.

I am one of those who believe that not every suicide is preventable. Isolated people die by suicide, homeless people die by suicide, people in relation to others hide their suicide intent or deny they are considering and/or planning to die by suicide, people who impulsively die by suicide may give little to no warning to allow an intervention to occur, not every patient in treatment because they are at risk for suicide is treated effectively, not every patient in treatment because they are at risk for suicide responds to our best efforts to help them. That said, many of those who become suicidal give us opportunities to prevent them from making a tragic and irreversible decision to die by suicide and to help reverse and redirect whatever is the death trajectory they may currently be on. For caregivers, this is the highest of our callings. For caregivers who treat those suicidal, the risk of a patient/client suicide happening on our watch and in spite of our best efforts is an occupational hazard we accept the minute we assume our care-giving role. Suicide happens.

And when suicide happens, caregivers have yet another role, that of potentially taking care of those we call survivors of suicide. As noted above, those bereaved by suicide are unwittingly and unwontedly thrust into contact with potential caregivers– EMTs and police, emergency department personnel, coroners, and medical examiners, etc.– and may willingly seek care-giving from a host of other available others: crisis workers, support group leaders and fellow survivors, counselors and therapists, etc. Each of us in these roles is in significant position to make the road to be travelled by survivors less burdensome, less dangerous, less symptomatic, and less acutely painful. The road they are on is a life course. The journey down that road need not be one accomplished without our support and help.

This book is a book of care-giving for caregivers. It is written and edited by caregivers who have walked the walk as both those who work with those bereaved by suicide and who have been intimately impacted by suicides of loved ones. In turn, they have gathered an octet of guest authors who individually and collectively offer a wealth of relevant experience to the reader. All told, the quilt they have woven for you is warm, comforting, and replete with enriched patterns of perspective and information that are enormously helpful to those who work with those bereaved by suicide.

It is an honor for me to have been asked to offer you this brief Foreword. I am in awe of my colleagues who have suffered the loss of a loved one to suicide and who, out of the potential rubble of that experience, have devoted themselves to doing all possible to support and work with others having shared similar experiences, no less doing whatever is possible to reduce the numbers who may yet share that fate. At last count, I have worked as a Suicidologist for the past 40 years. Over the course of my career, I have borne witness to the enormous impact the survivor community has head on clinicians, researchers, and others who, themselves, have not had the personal experience of survivorship. This book is one example, one terrific example, of just that kind of impact.

If you are reading this because you are contemplating purchasing this resource, do so now. If you are reading this because you have already made that decision and have started your reading here with my prefatory remarks, I thank you for so respecting Michelle's and John's decision to choose me to introduce them and their work to you. And I greatly thank you for giving care to those who are the subjects of this volume.

~ Lanny Berman, Ph.D., ABPP
Executive Director, American Association of Suicidology
President, International Association for Suicide Prevention

September 23, 2010

****

THE IMPORTANCE OF LANGUAGE

By Michelle Linn-Gust, Ph.D.

Editor's Note: Adapted from "The Language of Suicide and Grief" in *Rocky Roads: The Journeys of Families through Suicide Grief* by Michelle Linn-Gust, Albuquerque, NM, Chellehead Works, 2010.

The word *suicide* is one of the most emotion evoking words and topics there is. People have views from one end of the spectrum that suicide is selfish to the complete other end where people believe that one has the right to take his or her own life if one wishes to.

Before talking about suicide, one must understand the language around it because often it is the language that defines how people react to the topic. Plus it puts everyone on the same plane about what words define who and what. Suicide itself is the act of killing oneself although it is the words that describe what often are called the pillars of suicide (prevention, intervention, and postvention) and the people involved in a suicide that cause the confusion.

The study of suicide, known as suicidology, originated in the 1940s with Edwin Shneidman and three Los Angeles, California, colleagues: Norman Farberow, Robert Litman, and Mickey Heilig. The work that these four men began is what almost every piece of the three pillars of the field are built on. Prevention is everything that comes before even thoughts of suicide (also known as suicide ideation). This includes education: to teach people the warning signs to look for and what resources are available if they are worried about someone they care about.

Intervention is what Living Works Education (a suicide prevention training organization based in Canada) calls "suicide first aid or "suicide

CPR." It is identifying someone who is thinking about suicide or who might have a plan to attempt suicide and getting them help. Postvention is what comes after the attempt or the loss—it is helping the people who are left behind find hope again. And as Shneidman said, postvention after suicide is prevention for the next generation (Shneidman, 1972). By helping the bereaved through their losses, we support their efforts to find life-sustaining hope again. And by providing this support we are breaking the legacy of suicide in families.

Not so long ago the term *suicide survivors* was the accepted phrase in the United States for people coping with suicide loss. Shneidman coined the term *suicide survivors* in the 1960s. He used it to define anyone directly affected by a suicide, which usually included the immediate (and typically biological) family. As the movement gained momentum, this was the term used. It can be confusing, though, because attempters often consider themselves survivors of suicide.

Outside the United States, the typical term used is *bereaved by suicide,* which is a more appropriate way to describe someone coping with suicide loss. Ultimately, both attempters and people who are grieving a suicide death are survivors of suicide, but each group deserves its own name, and the term *survivors* better describes attempters. While we all seek to find hope again in our lives, we also need to feel we belong somewhere before we can move forward together.

The only possible issue heard with the term *bereaved by suicide* is that bereavement can have an expiration date. After people have been bereaved by suicide for many years, they may stop feeling bereaved. Perhaps they have moved to a new place along the journey. You will see several different words and phrases used to define people bereaved after a suicide loss in this book. Use the one that feels most comfortable to you.

Often, when discussing suicide, people will say that someone "committed suicide." Some cultures and religious denominations view suicide as something that goes against the natural order of life. People are not supposed take their own lives because it runs counter to what we are taught to believe, that life is something to be cherished. In many places, suicide was considered a crime until as recently as fifty years ago.

Criminalization or condemnation of suicide can be a deterrent. For some suicidal people the fear of committing a crime by ending one's life or the idea of going to a not-so-desirable afterlife is enough to discourage a lethal attempt at suicide. But for the bereaved, for the people left behind after the loss, the condemnation of suicide can stigmatize the event and make them feel afraid or embarrassed to seek help or admit how a loved one died. Depending on their values and beliefs, it can mean a loved one committed a crime or a sin.

There are other ways to convey that someone ended a life by suicide. For instance, I use *died by suicide.* It is simple and to the point. Some people use it as a verb: *she suicided.* Others will say that someone "completed suicide" although that raises the question of the number of times they attempted before they made a lethal attempt.

A word I choose never to use regarding either the person who died or the person who is bereaved: *victim.* The word *victim* takes away our strength. Even when we are discussing someone who died by suicide, I do not believe this was a weak person. He or she was coping with something that many of us will never quite understand. As for the bereaved, I believe people who are coping with a loss are strong people, traveling a road that not everyone will understand. *Victim* strips that away. People coping with suicide loss are survivors of a suicide loss, and everyone should use words that emit that strength.

Other words that I choose not to use are *closure, moving on,* and *recovery.* I do not believe that *closure* is a correct term for what we experience in suicide grief. That word makes it sound as if we close the book on a life that has ended and we place it in the bookcase, never to be opened again. That person remains with us for the rest of our lives, although in a different form. He or she still affects who we are. And the same with moving on. Yes, we move forward without them, but they are still with us because they helped form who we are, as their deaths affect who we become with the new choices in front of us. *Recovery* implies we will be the same person we were before the person died but we will have been transformed and become stronger in the process of grief.

Often we believe we know what grief is because of what we have viewed on television or in the movies. We could call this the propaganda of grief. Sometimes we see a parent who does not share his or her grief with a child, or we run into a person who chooses a self-destructive route through life, using the suicide as the excuse for those poor decisions. Experiences like this can hinder our own grief processes. It is important that we spend time educating ourselves on grief and how we can work through it.

According to Webster's Dictionary, *grief* is mental suffering or distress over loss; sharp sorrow; painful regret (1996). Through dissecting this definition we can learn volumes about grief. For instance, it might not always be about the death loss of a person in our lives. Sometimes we grieve the loss of an opportunity or a friend who has left our lives. But as we are using the word for the purpose of this book, it is sharp sorrow—the pain of someone dying can feel like the stabbing pain of something hurting us. And it can be full of painful regret that we were not there for the person and/or that we did not tell them how much we cared about them. *Grief* is the noun but *grieving* is the verb—the feeling and the journey we have embarked on after our loved ones have died.

Webster's defines *bereave* as to deprive, especially by death (1996). An example would be that we are "bereaved after suicide loss." *Mourning* is defined as the expression of sorrow (or grief) that one feels after someone has died. While these are the most basic words to describe the loss, they do not give the full picture of the loss we experience after a suicide.

One issue with the language of suicide is how often people believe they have to explain what they are saying. Some people are uncomfortable with describing what *survivor of suicide* or *suicidology* means. I have always looked at it as an opportunity to educate people about something of which everyone should be aware. The number of suicides in the world far eclipses the number of deaths attributed to many other causes. Everyone should have some understanding of suicide, and it is only through teaching people that we can make that possible.

Just as each person's journey is unique, so also will choosing the appropriate language to describe what he or she experiences individually. Some people will read the previous paragraphs and know exactly where they fit. Others will feel they are settling for something with which they do not completely agree. And yet others will search out other words, or choose none at all, to describe their emotions.

References

Shneidman, E. S. (1972). Foreword. In A. C. Cain (Ed.), *Survivors of suicide* (pp. ix-xi). Springfield, IL: Charles C. Thomas.

Webster's New Universal Unabridged Dictionary. (1996). New York: Barnes & Noble Books.

****

SETTING THE SCENE

By John Peters, M.Suicidology

It must be the ultimate question for philosophers– why should someone take his or her own life? Perhaps a deeper philosophical question is "Why do we *not* take our own lives?" Why have we always had suicide with us? Why have we had so many different attitudes to suicide over time and across different cultures?

We seem to spend so much of our energies maintaining our own life and the lives of others, even the creation of life involves the danger of pregnancy and childbirth– so why should people wish to take their own lives?

To illustrate the variety and contradictions in our attitudes to suicide we can look at some examples. Captain Oates walked to his death in a blizzard in Scott's Antarctic Expedition in order that his incapacity should not hamper the chance of his colleagues reaching safety. Almost every week we hear of the activities of "suicide bombers" who are willing to lose their lives in pursuance of their political objectives or to protect their religious beliefs. Some people may look upon these examples as heroes, others as villains. But why do we have quite different attitudes to these and other suicides?

If we look into the history of suicide we will see some of the social and cultural bases for our attitudes. The ancient Greeks tolerated suicide if there were worthy reasons, such as to avoid the shame of dishonor. This attitude was shared by the Romans but they took a very different attitude to slaves and soldiers who took their lives. The death of a slave would be a loss of property and the loss of a soldier would reduce the nation's fighting capabilities. These examples show the social and political reasons for attitudes to suicide.

Perhaps the first person to significantly put the study of suicide into the academic arena was the sociologist Emile Durkheim. He saw the study of suicide as a means of better understanding the structure of society. In his book *Le Suicide* (1897) he commented on the lower rates of suicide in the Catholic countries such as Spain, Portugal, and Italy in contrast to the higher rates in the Protestant countries such as Prussia, Saxony, and Denmark. However, he further noted that it was necessary to take into account that the social conditions in these countries could contribute to the differences. He took his argument further by comparing those German states that were predominantly Catholic, such as Bavaria, with those that were predominantly Protestant such as Saxony. He found similar differences when he looked at the suicide rates in Swiss cantons where he was able to differentiate those that were predominantly of one denomination. By this comparison within a nation with similar economic and other common circumstances he was able to reason that the difference in the suicide rates was influenced as a consequence of religious adherence. Durkheim's argument was that

The only essential difference between Catholicism and Protestantism is that the second permits free inquiry to a far greater degree than the first... So if Protestantism concedes a greater freedom to individual thought than Catholicism, it is because it has fewer common beliefs and practices. Now, a religious society cannot exist without a collective *credo* and the more extensive the *credo* the more unified and strong is the society.... Thus we reach the conclusion that the superiority of Protestantism with respect to suicide results from its being a less strongly integrated church that the Catholic church. (Durkheim, 1897/1951, pp. 157-159)

Durkheim also looked at the extent that we are integrated into the domestic society and also the degree of our integration into the political society. It is this author's view that the breakdown of relationships and whether or not the partners are married is a major risk factor in the incidence of suicide and too often overlooked by research. Anecdotal evidence also suggests that young men have particular difficulties with relationship breakdown.

It has been noted for some time that at times of war and other national difficulties the suicide rate falls. "As they force men to close ranks and confront the common danger, the individual thinks less of himself and more of the common cause" (Durkheim, p. 208). Recently it has been found that during the "Troubles" in Northern Ireland the suicide rate fell but since the problems there have significantly reduced, the suicide rate has risen again (University of Ulster, 2005).

Why have we spent so much time considering the work carried out over 100 years ago by an early German sociologist? We will see later that there are grounds to question aspects of Durkheim's conclusions, but we also can see the importance of external events that influence the decision to suicide. Suicide is a personal act but one that is influenced by a wide range of events and circumstances.

References

Durkheim, E. (1951). *Suicide: A study in sociology* (J. A. Spaulding & G. Simpson, Trans.; G. Simpson, Ed.). New York: Free Press. (Original work published 1897).

University of Ulster (2005). *Suicide Rates Up After the Troubles* *http://news.ulster.ac.uk/releases/2005/1806.html* (retrieved 30/09/2010).

****

LET'S LOOK AT THE FIGURES

By John Peters, M.Suicidology

The World Health Organization (WHO, 2010) summarizes the problem of suicide as follows:

Every year, almost one million people die from suicide; a "global" mortality rate of 16 per 100,000, or one death every 40 seconds.

In the last 45 years, suicide rates have increased by 60% worldwide. Suicide is among the three leading causes of death among those aged 15-44 years in some countries, and the second leading cause of death in the 10-24 years age group; these figures do not include suicide attempts which are up to 20 times more frequent than completed suicide.

Suicide worldwide is estimated to represent 1.8% of the total global burden of disease in 1998, and 2.4% in countries with market and former socialist economies in 2020.

Although traditionally suicide rates have been highest among the male elderly, rates among young people have been increasing to such an extent that they are now the group at highest risk in a third of countries, in both developed and developing countries.

Mental disorders (particularly depression and alcohol use disorders) are a major risk factor for suicide in Europe and North America; however, in Asian countries impulsiveness plays an important role. Suicide is complex with psychological, social, biological, cultural, and environmental factors involved.

When we look further into the figures we see wide differences from one country to another with significant differences over time and major gender differences.

One continuing problem in studying suicide statistics is the difficulty in being sure that the death is in fact suicide. In fact many deaths that are suicide are classified as accidental or as open verdicts. Steve Taylor (1982) conducted a study of people who met their deaths when they were hit by tube trains on the London Underground. Over a twelve-month period he found 32 cases where there were no strong clues as to the reason for the death. No suicide notes were left and no witnesses were able to state that the victim jumped deliberately. Of these 32 cases, 17 resulted in suicide verdicts, 5 were classified as accidental deaths, and 10 were open verdicts. We are reluctant to classify a death as suicide probably due to the continuing stigma (Taylor, 1982).

Selected countries: Suicide rates per 100,000 of population

Country	Last yr. records	M	F	Country	Last yr. records	M	F
Belarus	2003	63.3	10.3	Denmark	2006	17.5	6.4
Lithuania	2007	53.9	9.8	Germany	2006	17.9	6.0
Russia	2006	53.9	9.5	Canada	2004	17.3	5.4
Hungary	2005	42.3	11.2	U.S.A.	2005	17.7	4.5
Japan	2007	35.8	13.7	Australia	2004	16.7	4.4
Estonia	2005	35.5	7.3	Ireland	2007	17.4	3.8
Finland	2007	28.9	9.0	Norway	2006	16.8	6.0
Poland	2006	26.8	4.4	Netherlands	2007	11.6	5.0
France	2006	25.5	9.0	Spain	2005	12.0	3.8
Austria	2007	23.8	7.4	India	1998	12.2	9.1
China	1999	13.0	14.8	Italy	2006	9.9	2.6
CzechRep	2007	22.7	4.3	U.K.	2007	10.1	2.8
Romania	2007	18.9	4.0	Israel	2006	9.9	2.8
N.Zealand	2005	18.9	6.3	Greece	2006	5.9	1.2
Sweden	2006	18.1	8.3	Albania	2003	4.7	3.3

Source WHO World Health Statistics 2009

www.who.int/mental_health/prevention/suicide_rates/en/index.html

It might surprise many that the countries with the highest rates of suicide are those of the former Soviet Bloc. Three possible reasons can be put forward to explain this. Following Durkheimian theory we can suggest that the new society after the fall of communism has a less integrated structure leading to the second suggestion that there is a greater disparity of wealth and more unemployment. The third suggestion is that there has been a greater availability of cheap alcohol. The national governments have made arrangements to address this last problem.

The second notable feature of the table is that with the exception of China, every country has a significantly higher suicide rate amongst men than women. This always has been found in the history of suicide and perhaps it is the result of the more aggressive and risk-taking nature of men. The reason for a higher rate of female suicides in China has been attributed to the movement of men to the urban areas for work leaving the women at home where there is a ready availability of toxic agricultural chemicals.

The third feature that can be seen when we look again at Durkheim's expectation of Catholicism serving as a protective factor. For example the Republic of Ireland, a predominately Catholic country, now has a higher rate of suicides that its neighbor, the United Kingdom, which is predominately a Protestant country. It is interesting that Albania, although a former member of the Soviet Bloc, has a very low suicide rate which can be explained by the fact that Albania is the European country with the highest proportion of adherents to Islam. However, recent reports suggest that Albania faces an increase of suicides due to a lack of government interest and an attitude of shame towards suicide (Moka, 2008). Moka quotes Professor Edmond Dragoti– "Under communism, it was the government that assigned you a job, a profession, and a social status. This is something that the individual now has to invent on his own." So the preventative factor of the religion of Islam is countered by the breakdown of the certainty that the former communist state provided.

The overall suicide rates provide us with some insights into the causes of suicide, but these are crude assessments at a particular point in time. We can learn more when we look at rates of suicide that are differentiated by gender, age, and over a period of time. Firstly, we will examine the suicide rates in England and Wales (approximate population in 2010, 52 million) and later make some comparisons with the situation on Ireland and the U.S.A. Other countries could have been examined but this limited view should point to overall trends. These graphs give an immediate picture of a complex scene when we look at suicide statistics. Of immediate notice is the reduction of the rate of suicide in the older groups where both men and women show a significant reduction in the period under review (1968-2008). We previously viewed the older groups as the most at risk. This no longer applies in England and Wales. You will see that the over 65 men and women were formerly those most at risk but they are now only the third-placed group.

Reasons for this can include:

- Better medical support and new medication.
- Better hospice and other support for those not able to live independently.
- Better financial support including better pensions.

These are primarily social changes that give the older groups more confidence in their future and less hopelessness. Recent economic events may give us cause for concern that some of these improvements may be reversed.

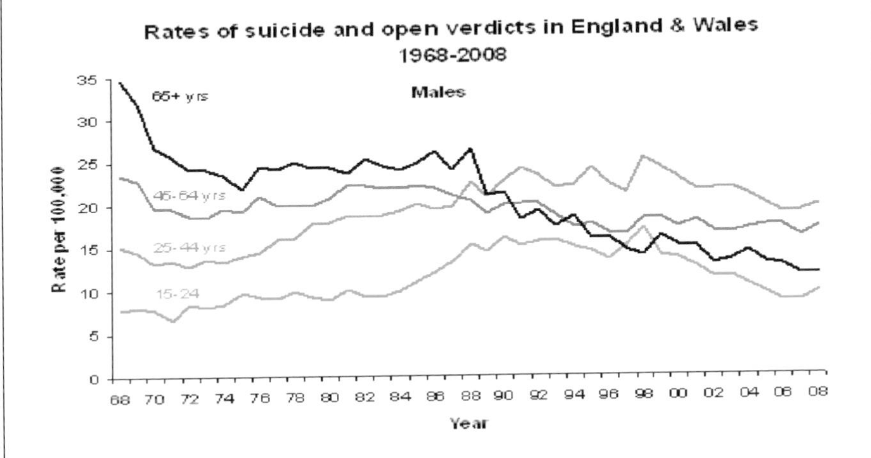

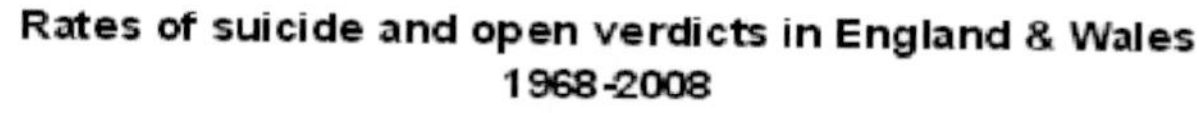

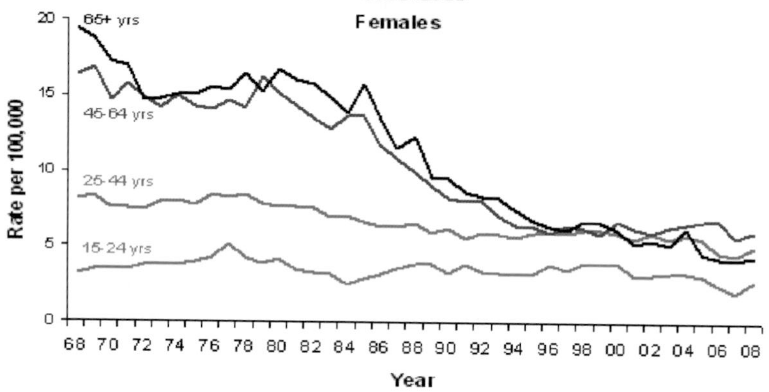

Oxford University Centre for Suicide Research
Data from Office of National Statistics *http://cebmh.warne.ox.ac.uk/csr/msui6808.html*

Much concern has been expressed in recent years at the rise in young male suicides. The graph shows this clearly but it also shows that a peak was reached in 1998 and has since fallen back. At the same time the rate of young female suicides has remained fairly constant over the period under review.

At the same time we have seen boys achieve poorer results at all levels of education relative to their sisters. I feel that this must be explained by the changing social conditions and the place of the young male in society. Many job opportunities have been lost, particularly in heavy industry and manufacturing and the young male who previously had a clear view of what lies ahead for him now has a very mixed picture of the future. That the young male rate has recently fallen may be seen as an acceptance of their new position in society and possibly also a regression to the mean.

It must be remembered that statistics such as the rates quoted above reflect the past and do not always predict the future. What we see from these tables is a reflection of changing circumstances in a particular country over a period of 40 years. It gives us some clues about suicide in the future but we must be very careful in our projection of the results into the future. It is also a warning that we need to use up-to-date figures when we comment on suicide rates. I still see comments that the trend in the rate of suicide in England and Wales is rising– it is not. And that the groups most at risk are the elderly– they are not. Finally, you will see that the very last figures do show a slight increase. Is this an indication that the credit crunch might be having an effect?

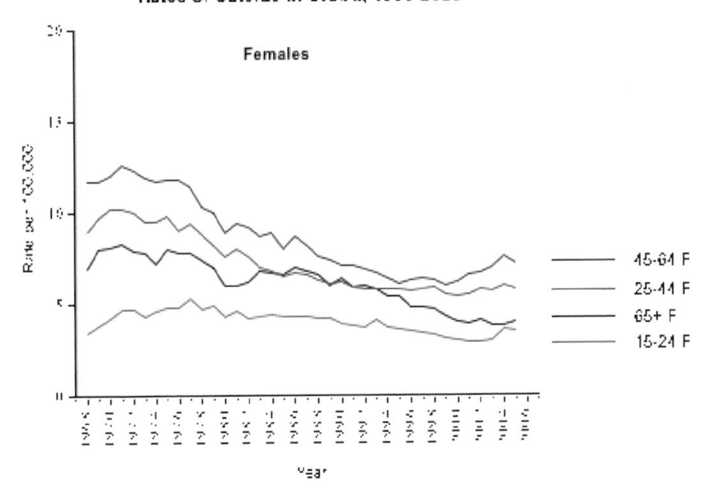

Suicide rates in the USA

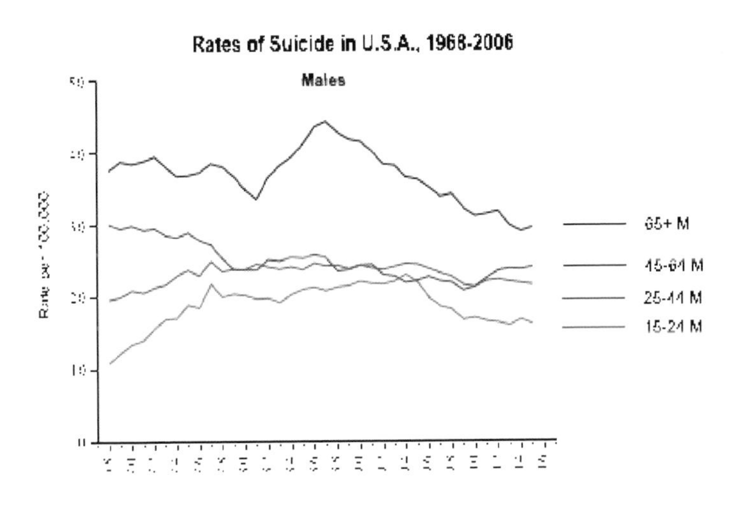

The graphs above show many similarities with those from England and Wales though the 65+ rates for women are surprisingly below the rates for 45-64 and for those 25-64. Overall, the younger women's suicide rates are fairly constant whilst the over 45 rates show consistent falls, probably due to the reasons we outlined earlier when discussing the reduction of older suicide rates in England and Wales.

Again the younger rates in the U.S.A. showed a disturbing increase in the first half of the period under review but have since fallen back. It can be conjectured that the same reasons of younger men having difficulty with the changing social and economic situation can be put forward as one explanation.

Perhaps the standout figures of the U.S.A. graphs are those of the over 65 men where there was a large initial rise followed by a significant fall in the rate since it peaked in 1987. Both sets of graphs are tending to show that the rates are converging and we need to be aware of this when we consider the problems of suicide.

Suicide rates in Ireland

It may be of value to look more closely at the difference between the suicide rates in Ireland in contrast with the U.K. The two countries have many cultural and historic similarities, but Ireland has a deep Catholic heritage. It should be noted that suicide was only decriminalized in Ireland in 1993 and the Catholic Church continues to have a major influence on legislation particularly in the fields of abortion and fertility treatment.

Suicide rates (per 100.000) - United Kingdom 1955 – 2004

1955	1960	1965	1970	1975	1980	1985	1990	1995	1999	2004
10.7	10.7	10.4	7.9	7.5	8.8	9.0	8.1	7.4	7.4	7.0

Suicide rates (per 100.000) - Ireland 1955 – 2004

1955	1960	1965	1970	1975	1980	1985	1990	1995	1999	2004
2.3	2.9	2.4	1.8	4.7	6.3	7.8	9.5	11.3	12.2	9.7

Ireland also has undergone a major economic surge since joining the European Union and this can be viewed in Durkheimian terms as to be expected as he envisaged suicide rate rise both at times of economic depression and also economic prosperity (Taylor, 1982). Care is needed in the interpretation of suicide recorded rates as the earlier low rates of suicide well may have been affected by the reluctance to classify deaths as suicide before suicide was decriminalized.

The effect of religion on suicide rates recently has been examined in detail based primarily on the European Values Survey (Cleary & Brannick, 2007). Whilst the attendance at Mass has fallen from over 90% in 1974 to 50% in 2003, Ireland still has a much higher level of church attendance (three times that of Britain and four times that of France). The EVS survey also found a rate of "belief in God" above 90% in both 1981 and 1999 with similar results for "belief in life after death" and "belief in Heaven" (Cleary & Brannick, 2007).

However, this continued support for the core beliefs of the Catholic Church has not held up in a number of the other areas surveyed. In the Attitude to Marriage survey, those who felt that marriage is an outdated institution had risen from 10% in 1981 to 20% in 1999 and those who felt that divorce is never justified had fallen from 50% in 1981 to 30% in 1999. So we can see from both Ireland and Albania that the protective factor is not the adherence to the religion *per se* but rather the extent to which the values of the faith are fully accepted.

References

Cleary, A. & Brannick, T. (2007). Suicide and changing values and beliefs in Ireland. *Crisis*, 28(2), 82-88.

Moka, B. (2008, August 11). Albania faces epidemic of suicides. BalkanInsight.com. *www.balkaninsight.com/en/main/features/12321/* (retrieved 30/09/2010).

World Health Organization. (2010). Suicide prevention (SUPRE). Retrieved, April 15, 2010, from *www.who.int/mental_health/prevention/suicide/suicideprevent/en/*.

****

Is Suicide Bereavement Different?

By John Peters, M.Suicidology

This is a question frequently posed by academics as well as those who may be offering support to bereaved survivors. The question has been addressed very clearly by Jack Jordan in his paper of the same name. In his literature review, Jordan finds that some research has found little difference, but stresses that the perception of survivors and clinicians who work closely with them are clear that there are marked differences. (Jordan, 2001).

Surprisingly, this is not a question that I am asked by those survivors who call our National Helpline in the UK of which I frequently man. Their question is more likely to be, "Why is suicide bereavement so much *harder* that other forms of bereavement that I have suffered?" These callers clearly recognize that there is a difference and many will make personal comparisons between previous losses and the suicide that is the reason for their call. Any form of bereavement is likely to be a difficult journey, but why is it so difficult in the case of suicide? I'm sure that many other forms of bereavement will be equally hard. I recently attended a meeting with those who had been bereaved by manslaughter or murder. I found it very difficult to imagine how I would cope with such a situation.

As Jordan (2001) points out, it might be that there are not *quantitative* differences between suicide survivors and those who have been bereaved by other causes, but there are *qualitative differences*. Many researchers have noted that suicide survivors struggle more with the questions that inevitably arise after the suicide.

The Centre for Suicide Prevention (Canada) (2001) in the article "Grief After Suicide" provides an excellent list of qualitative aspects that emerge from interviews including:

- A prolonged and intense search for meaning and the reason for the suicide (WHY?).
- A perceived need to deny the death.
- Feelings of being rejected by the deceased.
- Distorted notions of responsibility for the death and the ability to have prevented the suicide.
- A feeling of being blamed for causing the problems that began the suicidal ideation of the deceased.
- A perception of being stigmatized.

(References for each of the above are available in the "Grief after Suicide" article at *www.siec.ca*).

These aspects act as a very good starting point to illustrate the way that suicide bereavement is perceived by many as different.

The question "Why?" is a burning question for so many survivors and is certainly the question that I get asked most frequently when answering calls on our helpline. Difficult though it is to deal with the death of a loved one through illness, the loss through suicide poses many more questions and can challenge one's fundamental life values and beliefs. It makes one wonder what is the purpose of life?

The obvious and simplistic difficulty in trying to answer the "Why?" question is that the only person who knows all the answers is no longer with us. The next problem is that in many cases the person who decides to end his or her life will hide the intention. If you wanted to rob a bank would you tell the police of your intention? In the same way, many people who have decided to end their lives will not want others to interfere with their decision and this particularly applies to family and friends. It also will apply to professionals who may equally be misled by their patients into assuming that there is no problem. We also find that when the person is in the depth of their depression they are neither physically or mentally able to take the action that would end their life but when they "get better" they are able to do so. In some cases the very act of deciding that he or she will take his or her own life will be a relief and so the person may seem to be better. This puts those who care into a false sense of security and when the suicide occurs they will blame themselves for not realizing what the loved one intended. The number of cases when a suicide occurs in the day or two after discharge from a mental hospital should tell us that there is a particularly high risk at this time and discharged patients should be carefully monitored.

Amy Chow (2006) describes the concept of rejection very clearly. In fact she uses the term "abandonment" which I think is very appropriate. Because suicide is a self-inflicted way of death, the sense of abandonment and rejection is high and deeply felt.

Rejection of the care and concern of the survivors, often those who loved them most.

Rejection of facing problems that are now being dealt with in many cases by the survivors.

Rejection of the commitment to care for those left behind. This is felt particularly where children are left and the surviving partner or other family member (sometimes a grandparent) has to pick up the pieces.

Rejection of the opportunity to build the future together with the surviving members of the family.

Very often messages and hints are given to friends and family, but they may not be recognized at the time. Students have been known to give textbooks away to friends and others have made a special effort to emphasize their love for their friends and family. But it is only with hindsight that these messages can be understood, so we are angry with ourselves that we did not do enough to prevent the tragedy.

It may be a surprise to many that suicide survivors often have a perception that they are stigmatized. Jacqueline Cvinar (2005) in her literature review shows clearly that even today suicide survivors often have this perception of social stigma which she suggests is a remnant of the historical attitude to suicide when in many cultures those left behind after a suicide were asked to bear the additional loss of family property being confiscated and Christian burial being refused.

The remedy that was employed in many cases was to hide the fact that the person had died by suicide and invent an alternative explanation for the death. This stigma was very widespread and in some African cultures when a person is found to have hanged himself from a tree the tree is cut down and even the roots are burned. Even today we can hide the real reasons for the suicide and, whilst suicide is no longer a criminal act, it is too easy to find a verdict of depression or "while the balance of the mind was disturbed." But what caused the depression? We still shy away from the underlying reasons and some religious authorities are happier to deal with an explanation that the suicide was out of the control of the person and not a conscious decision.

Cvinar (2005) gives a more up-to-date reason for stigmatization in that she suggests that it is complicated by the social perception that the act of suicide is a failure by the deceased. As a result society blames the family for the loss on the survivors. William Worden (1991) explains that this puts added pressure on the relationships within the family unit. Cvinar (2005) concludes that the result is often the complete isolation of the bereaved survivor.

This will mean that whilst there is a great need for help, there also is often a greater reluctance by survivors to seek help. It also is less likely that survivors will easily find others who have been bereaved by suicide and many professionals may have had less or even no experience of dealing with suicide bereavement.

However an interesting proposition is made by Rudestan (1987) who suggests that there is a difference between *believing* one is stigmatized or negatively regarded by others versus *actually* being the object of negative appraisal. This illustrates a frequently found feature of the depression that follows a suicide– what the survivor **rationally** believes and what the survivor **emotionally** feels. This applies also to many other aspects of suicide bereavement support and illustrates the need to use therapeutic methods that will help the process of coping with the bereavement by rational thought.

Marilyn Hauser (1987, pp. 62-66) presents her interesting list of specific factors that lead to unresolved grief in suicide deaths:

- Suicide death is usually sudden and unexpected.
- Death by suicide is often violent.
- Suicide engenders guilt in the survivors.
- Suicide often occurs in systems already experiencing stress.
- Death by suicide can compromise usual mourning rituals.
- Suicide may lead to harmful expressions of unconscious anger and ultimately to distorted communication patterns.

Following a suicide some of the usual social supports may be withdrawn.

Even when there has been a previous suicidal attempt it most frequently still comes as a surprise to friends and family. Unlike a death from an illness the probability is that the person who was perfectly fit one moment is dead the next moment. Survivors will recall their loved one being perfectly well when they left them, perhaps to go to work, only to have a call from the police later in the day to tell of the suicide. The degree of shock can be profound in many cases.

In many cases there will have been many problems within the family or other systems that had an influence on the suicidal decision. Arguments and unfortunate events may have occurred and these situations may still be present within the family/system. I notice in calls to our helpline the high frequency of relationship breakdown as being a major reason for the suicide and most frequently I see it when a young man is not able to accept the rejection that he perceives following a relationship breakdown. This is in contrast to the stereotype of the young man who takes his relationships casually. It can literally destroy a young man when he feels he has been rejected in this way and see no reason to continue his life.

Anger is a frequently reported feature of suicide bereavement which is expressed in a variety of ways:

- We can be angry with ourselves (guilt).
- We can be angry with others (blame).
- We can be angry with the deceased but then feel guilty that we have expressed that feeling.

Most of us live in a blame society where we are more likely to consult a lawyer when anything goes wrong rather than dealing with the problem. So we blame, and even sue others, and the first in line for that blame may well be the health professionals who the bereaved feel are "responsible" for the death. This can be very unfair but has to be recognized as a reaction that many friends and family will feel. There is a danger that a primary reaction of staff may be to avoid litigation and avoid dealing with the family in case the wrong words are used. I would rather suggest that the professionals who supported the person before he/she died can be very helpful to the family if they are willing to make themselves available so that the family can know more details of the events before the death.

I frequently have calls where there is a great deal of antipathy towards the surviving partner, often after a relationship breakdown: "It was her fault." This situation can be very difficult where the couple have not married and the next of kin (in the U.K) are the parents of the deceased. I hear frequently of cases where a partner of many years is prevented by the parents of the deceased from attending the funeral. This series of events can make the grief journey very difficult. There can be particular difficulties where there are children of the partnership and can make it impossible for grandparents to have access to their grandchildren. It is so easy for relationships to breakdown after a suicide. In all cases, we should try to encourage contact between family members.

Anyone who is involved in suicide bereavement will realize that this is a difficult problem and that different people will grieve in different ways. We will expect to see many different forms of grief from different members of the family and friends and it is vital to recognize the differences and not expect all survivors to behave in a particular expected way.

References

Centre for Suicide Prevention. (2001). Grief after suicide. SIEC Alert #46. Available at *www.siec.ca.*

Chow, A. Y. M. (2006). *The day after: The suicide bereavement experience of Chinese in Hong Kong.* In C. L. W. Chan & A. Y. M. Chow (Eds.), *Death, dying and bereavement: The Hong Kong Chinese experience* (pp. 293-310). Hong Kong: Hong Kong University Press.

Cvinar, J. G. (2005). Do suicide survivors suffer social stigma: A review of the literature. *Perspectives in Psychiatric Care, 41*(1), 14-21.

Hauser, M. (1987). Special aspects of grief after a suicide. In E. J. Dunne, J. L. McIntosh, & K. Dunne-Maxim (Eds.), *Suicide and its aftermath* (pp. 57-70). New York: Norton.

Jordan, J. (2001). Is suicide bereavement different? *Suicide and Life-Threatening Behavior, 31*, 91-102.

Rudestam. K. E. (1987). Public perceptions of suicide survivors. In E. J. Dunne, J. L. McIntosh, & K. Dunne-Maxim (Eds.), *Suicide and its aftermath* (pp. 31-44). New York: Norton.

Worden, J. W. (1991). *Grief counseling and grief therapy.* New York: Springer.

****

HOW SUICIDE IMPACTS THE FAMILY

By Michelle Linn-Gust. Ph.D.

Editor's Note: Discussing how suicide impacts a family is a multi-layered topic. The section below only is a slice of how the family system is affected by a suicide. To read more in-depth information about how to help a family and its members after a suicide (including the individual relationships and information about how grief can differ for people depending on where they are in the lifespan), *Rocky Roads: The Journeys of Families through Suicide Grief* (by Michelle Linn-Gust, Chellehead Works, Albuquerque, NM, 2010) is a comprehensive resource. The information below was adapted by the author from that work.

What is a family?

To say someone is "family" is a tricky statement. Families are as unique as individuals. Defining the family in today's world is difficult because it can have such a wide range of meanings. What we called the traditional or nuclear family for many years does not exist as it used to. Families are not just mom, dad, and two kids. Instead, there are single-parent households, households where what we often called extended family (grandparents, aunts, uncles, cousins) live with a nuclear family, same-sex parent households, grandparents raising children, and the list goes on.

While there are several ways that families might be described, it ultimately is about how they describe themselves. What defines one family in one culture might be different in another. In some cultures (like the Navajo culture) someone might talk about a brother who someone in another culture would call a cousin. Some people are bound by DNA and blood while others do not feel they are a part of a biological family, but have instead found people elsewhere in their lives who are more important to them than their DNA-related relatives. And people have friends they call family.

For some families, there is a sense of shared resources beyond the simple biological connection. It could be psychological (healthy or unhealthy) or financial. People also might define family as those to whom they are most attached and feel most connected. A group of people might consider themselves a family because they live in one dwelling. They may live under one roof for economic reasons, or because that is what they do culturally. Someone might be living with a family because that person has no other family or place to go. And pets are considered members of the family more today than ever.

Beyond the people we call family whose lives are intertwined with ours, typically on a daily basis, we also have other communities in our lives we might call family. We could have a church family, a work family, or a neighborhood family. We might rely on each of these families for different kinds of support. Our church family helps us spiritually as well as giving us a social outlet at least once a week; our work family helps us through daily trials; and a neighborhood family is there for us to help watch our kids and loan us that egg when we need one more to bake a batch of cookies.

What happens in families after a suicide?

Once we take into account the many things that happen to us individually during grief, then we can step back and acknowledge what happens to the family. Looking at the family as a system, or a group, is important because the actions and reactions of each person affect the others—including the action of the person who died by suicide.

Yet why is it that some families are able to cope better than others after a loss, particularly a suicide? Why can some families experience a loss but seemingly move forward and "be okay" while others cannot quite function productively again? And why can some families move forward more quickly than others?

There are multiple answers to these questions. What affects a family as a unit is closely aligned with how a person copes after the loss of a loved one. Some of what affects how the family will cope was explained in a previous chapter on relationships, but here we will discuss more issues that might influence how the grief experience pans out.

Previous losses and how the family coped with them are one determinant for how a family will function. Families need to know their histories and how they have reacted to changes in the past. Change is difficult and loss brings a lot of change with it.

Suicide is not part of the normal course of family development. If it were, we would be better prepared to cope with it. A suicide will alter the family in ways that many people probably cannot predict.

Perceptions of the deceased loved one change after any death but in one complicated like suicide, they provide very different perspectives. Some family members might only remember the bad times with the person who died and be grateful they are gone. Other family members might feel sadness for the same reasons, sad that the person never took the chance on life he or she wanted them to have. Or some people may only remember the good. A child or teen in the home may remember the sibling being shuttled from hospital to hospital, yet all Mom and Dad can talk about is how wonderful the sibling was. It is important that people spend time working through some of the more difficult/sad memories because that can help them to deal with the definition of the death as a suicide. Once that process has been completed, the person can separate the life he or she shared with the loved one from how the loved one died.

When the deceased suffered from a mental disorder, the family might have revolved around that person and his or her problems. The family might have felt stigmatized for years and then even more shamed after the suicide, believing that people were saying that suicide was inevitable for the mentally ill person. It might not have been a mental disorder that someone suffered from; he or she simply may not have experienced the quality of life they wanted. Or the person did not want to burden the family anymore. The family might have feared that the person would die by suicide because of the pain they felt from the illness. The family might have already suffered a loss with the deceased when the illness was diagnosed. For parents who have children who suffer from any disability, at diagnosis they realize their children will never have the lives they hoped for when they brought them into the world. They suffered one loss with the child's illness, and the suicide is another.

A high level of trauma can accompany the suicide grief experience when the death is a shock or a surprise. But as the previous paragraph points out, suicide is not always unanticipated. More likely, that anticipation is not acknowledged in families. And this reality can cause further division in families as some members will wonder why they were not asked to help the person who died.

Loved ones can live in fear of the possible suicide of someone they care about. After an attempt, or during the ideation (when someone is thinking about suicide), family members often are removing possible methods a person might use to kill him or herself and keeping a vigilant eye out for the loved one's behavior. But deep inside them, they know that they cannot control all that a loved one chooses to do. For these families, when a suicide happens, they knew that it was not a matter of if but rather when the person would die (Maple et al., 2007).

When the loved one has died by suicide but also killed people before turning a method on himself (called homicide-suicide), family members will find themselves in a quandary for support. Often, the people who lost loved ones through the murder will not feel sympathetic to the suicide survivors, believing that their loved one deserved to die because he or she took another life (or lives) away.

When homicide-suicide happens, a father might kill his wife and then kill himself, possibly leaving a group of children without parents. The children may then be shuttled off to grandparents who might have a different view of suicide, one stuck in the heightened stigma of society in generations past.

Suicide can be the ultimate betrayal in a family. Family members think they have open and honest relationships with each other, and when the person dies, they feel as if that trust has been violated.

Some family members do not have an opportunity to say goodbye to the loved one. This can happen for a variety of reasons. There are family members who cannot return for the funeral or memorial. While these often are difficult times for families, they also can be times where families come together and are able to talk through the loved one's life and what led to the suicide. Family members who cannot attend the mourning rituals should find a way to cope with the details, perhaps by contacting loved ones and talking through the loss with them. However, there also are loved ones who are denied the opportunity to say goodbye. This could be because the family member is not told about the death. Perhaps the family was estranged from this person in some way.

If this happens, the family member who has been kept from the funeral needs additional outlets to cope with the loss. This could be through other family members and/or friends. Finally, children and teens sometimes are not allowed the opportunity to attend a funeral and/or memorial. They always should be given the choice to go. If they choose not to, it's okay, but the choice should be theirs. No matter what happens, family members all should have an opportunity to say goodbye to the loved one. This is only one step on the journey, but saying goodbye allows us to move forward with grief.

There is one theory that gives a good description of what happens in a family after a loss and describes a family after a suicide loss, too. The Integrated Individual-Family Model (Moos, 1995) discusses both the individual and family unit pieces of grief.

Changes in who talks to whom and in what way

After a suicide, everything changes; there is no doubt about that. There is a sense of "no holds barred" in families after suicide as well. If there was anger, or anything else lingering below the surface, this is when it comes out, typically with a vengeance. But it also can mean that family members who have not relied on each other before find they need one another for emotional survival.

People find out a lot about their families after a suicide. Sometimes they find out what they didn't know was going on with their loved one. They realize that some members of the family knew all the details while others did not. The older the person who died, the more people are involved (as people marry, etc.), and the situation can become more complicated.

Reconnection or cutoff of certain family members

Some family members will be angry at others for not being around (physically and/or emotionally) for the one who died. They might blame one person for the death and cut that person out of the family. If the suicide scares a family member, that person may cut him or herself out of the family, maybe not physically but emotionally (or both). Such a withdrawal may happen because the one family member that the person felt closest to is the one who died, or simply because the person can't handle the suicide itself and how it has changed the family.

It's possible that some family members will reconnect after the loss, that they will take this time to come back together after they have been emotionally apart for a long time. They will realize that they have lost one member and do not want to lose any others, or recognize how precious time is and that anyone could die on any day. This mostly appears to happen when aunts and uncles reconnect, or even connect for the first time, with the nieces and nephews of the sibling who died. They know they have the opportunity to keep their sibling alive for the children through the memories and do not want to miss that.

Confusion in family roles
(who is in charge and who has what responsibilities)
Children are particularly affected by this kind of confusion. Often their parents are too devastated by the loss of a child or a spouse to remember the rest of the family. No one forgets their surviving children on purpose; they just cannot see beyond the hole that the death has punched in their lives.

Parents also might fear disciplining a child because they do not want to upset the child. Grief makes us do things we would never have expected to do; we never can predict how it will make us act. By not disciplining children. parents may reinforce troublesome behavior, when the misbehaving children are simply looking for someone to acknowledge that they are there and that there is some normalcy, although it never will be the same as it was before the loved one died.

Overprotecting each other
This happens in several situations. While some parents might not discipline their children, others will be afraid to let them out of their sight because they do not want anything to happen to them. Children who know more about what happened to a sibling (through their relationship or through school) might not share with their parents details that they fear will hurt the parents. They do not want their parents to hurt more than they already are.

Parents who know details might not share them with their children, or even their spouse. This is done not to hurt them but to keep them from being hurt more. Parents, for example, sometimes change the story about how the person died. They do not want anyone hurt.

Sometimes one person might be the only one to know it is a suicide while all the other family members are led to believe it was something else (like an accident). While this ultimately hurts the family members who are not told (because they usually will learn the family secret eventually), it also hinders the grief process of the person who knows it was a suicide because that person cannot share it with anyone else.

Even though suicides are not covered up as they once were , people sometimes do change the story despite what is typed on the death certificate. This too is not done in malice or to hurt anyone; people erroneously believe that by covering it up, they are saving themselves and the family members a lot of grief and difficulty coping. What they do not realize is that it actually has just the opposite effect. I know of one woman who was told, in her teen years, that her mother died of cancer. She found out in her thirties that it actually was a suicide. Suddenly, she had to re-grieve her mother's death all over again, this time as a suicide. I am sure that the family members only wanted to protect her, never realizing they would ultimately cause her more pain.

Overprotecting also happens in support groups, particularly when adult children come with their parents. They might sit next to their mother and when each person in the group says who they lost and a little bit about their story, the adult children might not speak or might say very little. Sometimes they know something about the person who died, or the suicide, but do not want to share it because they do not want the parents to hurt more than they already are.

Family becoming isolated from friends and support network
I felt as if we were living in a bubble when my sister Denise died. Sometimes we seemed to be looking out of the bubble at everyone asking, "Why won't you all talk to us?" and everyone else was looking in saying, "We don't know what to say." That bubble was the house we lived in, and everyone else was gathered outside looking at us, many too upset to speak, and others too afraid to speak.

The systems perspective is important here. The family system feels separated from the outside environmental system (the community which is known as the suprasystem). Suicide can act as a wedge that comes between the family and the friends and support network. The issues surrounding suicide in general (like the shame and stigma) coupled with the family's embarrassment that it happened to them cause the isolation. There are times, too, when a family will isolate itself, not even realizing what it is doing. This is a coping mechanism, even if not an effective one, and might be the only one that the family (or members of the family) knows.

Suicide often involves mental illness, sometimes manifested in drug and alcohol abuse. For many years, the family might have hidden behind closed doors, not wanting anyone to see what really was going on in the house. I have heard stories of people who dressed family members to make them appear to be at least half functioning when people came over. Other families have hidden their loved ones, afraid of embarrassment by their actions.

These families can be described as closed systems. Their fear is what keeps them from reaching out. They do not want anyone to know what's really happening. When there is a suicide, they might try to cover it up, not wanting to add to the stigma already attached to the family because of one family member. They might fear opening the system lest everyone find out that the appearances are not what they seem.

Other families feel relief from the death and, while they may have to cope with their guilt, they also may finally open the curtains in the house, letting everyone see what happened now that there is no reason to cover it up. These families will be the most receptive to help but will need time to unravel the issues in which they have been wrapped up for years.

Some families might have more than one mentally ill family member, and that other family member will need more support following the suicide.

Relationships to the person who died will affect how a suicide is grieved. Was everyone getting along well when the person died? If the person who died was not functioning well, there may have been ongoing or unresolved arguments. Such festering wounds can leave the loved ones with extra guilt that the last conversation had been angry. Some people might not have been physically and/or emotionally present in the relationship either because of business in their own lives (this is particularly true for adult siblings who have families of their own beyond their birth family) or a strained relationship with the one who died.

If the relationship was strained, it will make the grief process more difficult. There will be more roads to travel to process the relationship and learn how to let go what cannot be changed because of the words said (or the words that were *not* said).

Even if a relationship was fairly good before the suicide, grieving a suicide death is not simple because everyone has to cope with his or her own issues that may or may not even relate to the person who died. Issues that might not relate to the death include abandonment or fear of being alone. When a loved one dies, those fears come through and need to be coped with separately from the death.

For instance, a wife whose husband kills himself might have abandonment issues that go back to her relationship with her parents although they have nothing to do with her husband (yet they might have caused some tension in her relationship with her spouse). When her husband killed himself, she felt abandoned by him although his suicide might have had nothing to do with her (and everything to do with fears about his own life and failures). She will have to cope with these issues as well as grieve the fact that he died by suicide.

What else is going on in a person's and a family's life when there is a suicide? Is it a difficult time because of job loss, marital difficulties, school exams, moving, or any other potentially stressful event(s)? The reality is that life is never devoid of stress, particularly stress that causes tension, depression, and sleeplessness. As I age, I believe that half of what life is about is coping with stress (and the other half is about learning to communicate with people). When someone dies by suicide, we have to add another level of stress to our plates as we try to comprehend the loss of a loved one by suicide. For some people, this can be a breaking point, so finding extra support at this time (or alleviating some stress by eliminating situations that are causing stress, if possible) is crucial.

But there also could be good things going on in one's life at this time. A woman could be planning her wedding when her father kills himself. She had planned for him to walk her down the aisle, and now he will not be there to do that for her. She might be devastated by this, and even believe he purposely hurt her by missing her wedding although his suicide had nothing to do with her. She will have to find resolution for her wedding. It will not be the same but maybe her brother will walk her down the aisle and maybe a candle can be lit for her father in recognition that while he is not there, he is still part of her family and her important day.

Are there other losses in a family's history? Some families do not have a long history together. They might be very young families (maybe only two people who have just married) or blended families that are created when two parents come together with several children. In some families, one side might have experience with loss and the other might not. There might not be any past loss, or this death might be one of several. Whatever the family's history is, it is important to consider earlier losses because they will help determine how the family will react to the suicide.

It also is important to look at not only how the family coped with past losses, but also how the family copes with stress. Does the family have coping skills that are productive? The family may be able to find help more easily if they can identify what they have been through previously. I realize this is easy for me to say but not so easy to accomplish. Usually there is one family member who is aware of this kind of information because that person has processed it and thought about it before. It is not always one of the parents; it could be one of the children (although more likely an adult child than an adolescent).

While any type of past loss will help determine the family's reaction to the suicide, so will knowing if there are suicides in the family's history. There is a genetic component to suicide and when suicide becomes part of one's vocabulary in what I call "a close and personal way," there is the reality that if it happened once, it could happen again. As we often say, we have to break the legacy of suicide in families.

When there is a suicide in a family, not all members are going to tell the same story around it. Remember that game "telephone" that starts out with one person whispering one sentence to the next person? By the time the sentence gets whispered to the person at the end of the line, it is totally different. We all see, hear, and understand things differently. Our perspectives are different, and that is why we can't walk in each other's shoes.

If you lined up a bereaved family and asked each of them to say what they believed happened to the deceased family member, my guess is that they would each tell you something slightly different. Each one had a different relationship with the loved one who died, and our perspectives are unique to each of us. We must honor and respect that in each of our family members.

Elderly people have a higher rate of suicide than many other age groups. A grandmother could die of natural causes and the grandfather, not wanting to be alone, might follow with a suicide, wanting to rejoin his loved one. The family left behind has suddenly lost both its matriarch and patriarch at one time and must digest two significant losses in a short period of time. Or an aging parent who is dying of a terminal illness might arrange his or her death so he or she does not have to endure a long, painful death. This can be difficult for some family members to accept even though the grandparent is at peace with it, a combination that causes friction when some family members accept this choice while others do not.

Because of financial difficulties, families are sometimes forced to move in with relatives, and those relatives might have different views about suicide. Maybe they never liked the person the surviving partner was married to and will let the spouse and children know now that the person has died. If a spouse dies, the surviving spouse might eventually remarry, once again causing change, particularly for the children.

Cracks in families run deeper after suicide. The cracks need tending, whether by filling them with concrete or encouraging them to grow flowers. Everything that was going on should be explored as that will help the family understand where it needs to start to heal.

Because loss tests everything about us—our values, our patience, our relationships—we probably learn more about our family members, good or bad, during this time than at any other time in our lives. The crucial part is how we process what we learn and use it to make our families strong again.

References

Maple, M., Plummer, D., Edwards, H., & Minichiello, V. (2007). The effects of preparedness of suicide following the death of a young adult child. *Suicide and Life Threatening Behavior*, *37*, 127–134.

Moos, N. L. (1995). An integrative model of grief. *Death Studies*, *19*, 337–364.

****

THE IMPACT OF BEREAVEMENT BY SUICIDE ON CHILDREN AND ADOLESCENTS

By Michelle Flood, D.Ed Psych

"Telling must be a process. Not an event. For the tale will need to be retold and retold, and for virtually all, understanding will be repetitively reshaped as influenced by development, life experiences and accrual of new information about death" (Cain, 2002, p. 135).

Cain highlights four important aspects of bereavement by suicide during childhood or adolescence; young people do grieve; young people require developmentally appropriate support as they grieve; clear communication is necessary to facilitate the grieving process; and grief may be revisited as young people develop cognitively and psychologically.

Although earlier literature seemed to dismiss grieving in children, bereaved children and adolescents have been found to be vulnerable to psychological, cognitive, emotional, behavioral, and social difficulties. Bereavement by suicide may lead to further complications in the grieving process for children and adolescents as they are forced to re-evaluate their understanding of life.

This chapter aims to discuss the impact of bereavement by suicide on children and adolescents. It is based on the author's professional knowledge and experience in the area of Educational Child and Adolescent Psychology. The influence of family grief on individual members also is discussed. The topics covered in this chapter aim to inform all professionals, volunteers, and members of the public who come in contact with children and adolescents bereaved by suicide.

The Psychological Impact of Bereavement by Suicide on Children & Adolescents
Children and adolescent survivors of suicide present with behavioural difficulties, suicide ideation, depression, and symptoms of posttraumatic stress symptom. Adults involved with children and adolescents would benefit from being able to identify some of these symptoms. Markers for depressions include irritable mood; loss of interest in activities; loss of energy and appetite; feelings of worthlessness; and difficulty concentrating on everyday tasks (APA, 2000).

Posttraumatic stress symptoms in children are more difficult to identify as some of the symptoms found in adults are representative of normal childhood development, for example diminished interest in an activity (a symptom for the diagnosis of PTSD in adults) is common among children as they progress through the developmental stages. However, avoidance of places or events that are associated with the death, re-enactments of activities surrounding the death, and hyper-vigilance, manifesting in a lack of sleep, anxiety, and increased cardiovascular activity have been reported in children who experienced a trauma (Perry & Azad, 1999).

The Role of Development during Bereavement
There is a mutual relationship between bereavement and development; the young person's stage of development influences his or her grief at each stage and the bereavement influences and shapes his or her development.

Developmental Influences on Bereavement
Cognitive development limits a child's understanding of the three main characteristics of death; irreversibility, inevitability, and universality. A young person's understanding of death is explained here in terms of Piaget's stages of cognitive development (Piaget, 1960).

An infant will not be able to understand the concept of death however the infant will notice the separation from a significant adult. This may in turn have a negative effect on attachment, which can lead to emotional and behavioral difficulties throughout childhood and adolescence (Bowlby, 1963).

A child in early childhood (around three to five years) begins to form an understanding of death but may view death as reversible. Children at this stage of development may engage in magical thinking and sometimes believe that the death occurred as a result of something he or she thought. This explains the guilt that children are found to experience following the suicide death of a loved one. Children may become preoccupied with death and this may be evident through their play. It is likely that children will be concerned with the concrete details of the death and deceased, such as where the body is.

Children begin to understand that death is irreversible during middle childhood (around six to eleven years) and can happen to everyone. They may personify death and continue to engage in magical thinking in an attempt to change, undo, reverse, or take revenge (Dyregrov, 1998). Children may view death as a punishment. They may seek to identify with the deceased and may engage in imitative and disruptive behaviors.

Young people entering puberty and adolescence begin to engage in abstract thinking and therefore have a greater understanding of the motivation and the social stigma surrounding suicide. Adolescents' schoolwork may deteriorate and they may demonstrate poor concentration and motivation. Adolescents understand that the dead body is non-functional and that death is universal and irreversible. This greater understanding may leave adolescents more vulnerable to psychological distress, leading to imitative suicidal behaviors, while children's limited understanding may act as a buffer from the negative effects of death. Children's limited tolerance of emotional pain may force them to engage in magical thinking, which may act as a protective factor. However, in other ways children may be disadvantaged. For example, their limited vocabulary may prevent them from making their feelings known to others. Boyd-Webb (1993) suggested that children aged five to seven years may find the grieving process particularly difficult as they have some understanding of the irreversibility of death, yet do not have the social skills necessary to help them work through their understanding. Children may act out in an attempt to get adult attention to alleviate their suffering.

It is important to remember that children reach developmental milestones at different ages. This may be due to the interaction between social, biological, psychological, and cognitive development. Previous experience affects understanding of future events. Children who have had past experience with death have been found to have a more developed understanding of death than those who have not had such an experience (Clunies-Ross & Lansdown, 1988, cited in Ayyash-Abdo, 2001).

Social development may influence the impact of the suicide death on a young person. The death of a peer may be more traumatic for an adolescent than for a child as peers are usually more influential during adolescence than earlier childhood. Children and adolescents often do not like to stand apart from their peers and therefore they may not like to talk about the death and bereavement in front of their peers; however it is important that young people do not feel isolated and unable to identify with others their age. Therefore, having the opportunity to speak with other young people who have also been bereaved by suicide is a valuable source of support for suicide bereaved children and adolescents.

As children and young people develop cognitively and socially they may readdress their grief. Young adolescents who lost a parent or sibling during early childhood will have the ability to reinterpret the loss and its meaning throughout life. This is particularly true of a death by suicide as young people may struggle with the concept of a loved one taking his or her own life and feelings of anger and abandonment may resurface. As adolescents' social systems widen and they meet people who do not know of their loss it might be difficult for them to discuss their experience of suicide bereavement; this may affect the formation of emotional bonds and relationships. During important life-stage transitions, such as entry into puberty and school graduations it is likely that young people will be forced to acknowledge the person missing from their life. Therefore, people should be mindful that grief may re-emerge many years after the death.

The Impact of Bereavement on Development

Losing a loved one to suicide often influences a young person's bereavement trajectory. Children and adolescents may have to take on new roles within the family to fill the role previously held by deceased family member or to accommodate the grief of other family members. This may be particularly true for a young child who is bereaved by parental suicide. The child may be forced to 'grow up' quicker as the surviving parent may be unable to give the same level of practical or emotional support as they provided before the death.

Young children have been reported to regress developmentally after the death of a loved one; this is their attempt to cope with their loss. People dealing with four- to six-year-old children may witness toddler tantrums and enuresis following a death.

Suicide bereaved adolescents often adopt a new life perspective; they may no longer be interested in the mundane complaints and interests of their peers. Adolescents often withdraw from their peers in the aftermath of the death; potentially having long-term consequences for the adolescent's friendship network.

The Impact of Communication on Bereavement

As Cain (2002) outlined, clear and repetitive communication is required to facilitate the grieving process for young people bereaved by suicide. Children benefit from being told the truth about the nature of death (Nelson & Frantz, 1996). Children generally know more than adults presume and in the event that they are not told the truth, they will manufacture their own version of truth; one that often implicates them in the death. Adults working with suicide-bereaved children can assist their caregivers in this task by listening to the children's questions and answering as fully and concisely as possible. Simple, unambiguous language should be used. The permanency of the death should be explained; phrases such as "gone to sleep" are unhelpful; firstly the child may presume the loved one will wake up and, secondly, if the child understands the permanency of the loss they may be afraid that they themselves or other family members will disappear during their sleep. Processing the death is an ongoing task for children and young people and they may ask repetitive questions to reach an understanding. They benefit from being allowed to openly discuss their thoughts and concerns.

Bereavement Following the Suicide Death of a Parent, a Sibling, or a Peer

Parent

Children who lose their parent to suicide lose an attachment figure. This affects their psychological and social development. Their attachment to their surviving parent also may be affected, due to the parent's changing parenting style or to the child's changing perception of the surviving parent. Attachment related difficulties are similar in many ways to the traits demonstrated by children with Autism Spectrum Disorder (ASD) such as impaired social interaction skills. Children may find it difficult to start and maintain friendships. They may find it difficult to trust others. Attachment difficulties can be alleviated with appropriate interventions and teachers and other adults play an important role in bringing these difficulties to the attention of the appropriate professionals.

It is important that the child's attachment with the deceased parent is maintained. The child's surviving parent and other adults, such as a teacher, can facilitate this by encouraging open discussion about the child's relationship with the deceased parent and by remembering the parent's birthday and other important occasions.

Sibling
When a young person dies, the family composition is permanently changed. The order of the surviving siblings change, for example a sibling may become the oldest or youngest child in the family. Bereaved siblings have discussed the difficultly with answering the routine question: "How many brothers and sisters do you have?" The nature of the sibling relationship before the suicide death may impact the grief experienced; a sibling who was particularly close to the deceased may feel abandonment or guilt that he or she should have noticed something, a sibling who had an ambivalent or argumentative relationship with the deceased may feel he or she contributed to the death.

Peer
Adolescents are particularly affected by the suicide death of a peer. Reports of suicide clusters among this age group are all too common. Whether this is due to the heartbreak of losing a close friend or to the ill-considered desire to receive the attention received by the deceased is unclear. Adolescents are especially vulnerable to copycat behavior given their desire for conformity and peer acceptance. School staff and other youth workers can strive to reduce this copycat behavior by avoiding glamorizing the original death. Adolescents should be allowed to mourn their peer but in a way that avoids hysteria; rituals following the death should mirror those following a death by an accident or illness.

The Impact of Family Grief on Children and Adolescents
It is important to consider not only the child or adolescent's individual experience but that of the entire family system. The degree to which the young person can process his or her grief will be affected by the grief and behavior of the family. Parents' perceptions of their child's understanding of the death will influence the level of openness with which feelings and thoughts are discussed. Open communication is vital to the achievement of positive family functioning. A young child can only access professional support through the parent; it may be necessary for others to encourage a parent to recognize the need for such support. The young person may strive to make sense of other family members' grief, potentially believing it to be harder for others than themselves and thus

taking on a protective role. It is important that in relationships rules and boundaries maintain continuity, while at the same time being flexible, to facilitate the young person reaching a place where he or she can move forward with his or her grief. This has relevance for all the systems of which the young person is a part, including school, sports clubs. And so forth.

Conclusion

This chapter sought to present findings from research and practice on the impact of a death by suicide on surviving children and adolescents. The experience is life changing and it is clear that professionals and other adults that come into contact with suicide bereaved young people have a role in easing the pain for this vulnerable group.

When interacting with young people bereaved by suicide, adults should look out for:

- Symptoms of posttraumatic stress symptoms and depression
- Attachment related difficulties
- Attribution of blame to self for a role in the death
- Risk of neglect by caregivers

Avoid causing added distress by:

- Drawing attention to the young person in front of his or her peers
- Asking questions about family composition
- Consider developmental requirements and their impact on the young person's grief
- Consider changing relationships with peers and the impact of this on the young person's well being
- Consider the long-term implications of grief such as earlier grief resurfacing at life-stage transitions
- Be mindful of the young person's repetitive need to discuss and process the death
- Consider the changing relationships within the family and the impact of this on the young person
- Avoid glamorizing the suicide death of a peer
- Maintain continuity of rules and boundaries, but facilitating adaptability as necessary

References

American Psychiatric Association. (2000). *Diagnostic and statistical manual of mental disorders DSM-IV-TR (4th ed.).* Washington DC: Author.

Ayyash-Abdo, H. (2001). Childhood bereavement. What school psychologists need to know. *School Psychology International, 22*, 417-433.

Bowlby, J. (1963). Pathological mourning and childhood mourning. *Journal of the American Psychoanalytic Association*, 11, 500-541.

Boyd-Webb, N. (Ed). (1993) *Helping bereaved children: A handbook for practitioners.* London: Guilford Press.

Cain, A. C. (2002). Children of suicide: The telling and the knowing. *Psychiatry, 65*, 124-126.

Dyregrov, A. (1998). *Grief in children: A handbook for adults.* London: Jessica Kingsley.

Perry, B. D., & Azad, I. (1999). Post-traumatic stress disorder in children and adolescents. *Current Opinions in Pediatrics, 11*, 310-316.

Piaget, J. (1960). The general problems of the psychobiological development of the child. In J. M. Tanner & B. Inhelder (Eds.), *Discussions on child development: Proceedings of the World Health Organization study group on the psychobiological development of the child* (Vol. IV, pp. 3–27). Edinburgh: Tavistock.

****

SUICIDE BEREAVEMENT IN THE WORKPLACE

By Emily Duval, M.A. Psychology, MBACP (Accred)

A death by suicide can resonate throughout a survivor's life, including one's place of work. Managers have a duty of care to recognize the needs of those who have been recently bereaved and should be made aware that following a suicide, survivors are considered at risk and may require additional support. News of a suicide is both shocking and profoundly devastating at once. From the first moment staff are informed of the suicide, the manner in which employers handle the situation matters a great deal, and can affect the grief response and overall healing process.

When a death by suicide impacts a work environment, it is essential for colleagues to understand that grief after suicide is complex. Guilt, shame, rejection, and blame are common features. Survivors often feel isolated in their grief because of the stigma attached to suicide.

Suicide is not limited to any particular status or seniority. It happens to all levels of managers, senior executives, directors, support staff, specialists, clerks, housekeeping, porters, drivers, etc. Any person with even semi-regular contact with the decedent can be affected by the death, and that includes customers and the general public.

For colleagues or supervisors who were not close to the deceased, but responsible for delivering the news and managing the aftermath in the workplace, appropriate support should be offered by the employer.

Witnesses who discover the scene, but were unknown to the deceased, may experience symptoms of trauma: flashbacks of disturbing images, nightmares, avoidance, hypervigilance, etc. This population also must be given consideration for additional support and time off, if necessary.

While some suicides take place at work, they may not be work-related. Conversely, work-related suicides may occur at the work site, or elsewhere. Each of these creates a complex situation resulting in a range of reactions from loved ones and work colleagues.

If an employee has died by suicide, companies should use open and honest communication at appropriate times in a safe setting to inform staff.

Sharing my own experience:

When my boyfriend died by suicide in May 1993, we worked for the same company. He had been dismissed the previous week. I was working on a Sunday, having just seen him on Friday, we had made plans to review his CV. All day throughout my shift I had been thinking about him, hoping he wasn't feeling too depressed about losing his job, remaining optimistic that he would find other work before long.

At the end my shift, my team and I crowded into the sign-out room as usual. It was in this shoe-box sized space that our supervisor decided to pull me aside into a corner and tell me the news about my boyfriend's suicide. She told me it happened Friday. I was standing up – there was nowhere to sit and nowhere else to look except at her or the wall. The room was still crammed full of staff stumbling around each other, eager to sign themselves out and get on with their evenings. From what I remember, the supervisor didn't offer any words of condolence or ask if I felt okay about driving. My knees went wobbly and my head felt hot. In an effort to stay composed, I actually thanked her for telling me before I shuffled out to my car in a stupor. By that time, the rest of my colleagues had left the building. I managed to drive to my boyfriend's flat where I found his best friend who was able to fill in the details of what happened on Friday. Evidently, an ambulance arrived to the flat where my boyfriend was alone and dying. The emergency medical staff were unable to locate a telephone book to inform anyone, however, they did find some bit of paper with information of his recent employer, thus how it came to be that the company received– and subsequently delivered– the news.

In my case, it only was several months after the death that I reflected on how the news was communicated to me. I realized that informing someone of a suicide was not routine for this particular manager and she probably didn't have the slightest idea of how to approach it with sensitivity. She could have benefited from some support and guidance herself. I believe that any company has a duty of care for staff, especially when imparting this type of information.

Where possible, staff should be informed of the suicide in a comfortable, safe atmosphere where people can sit down, if needed. Having a member of HR on-hand to show presence may be advisable, however, it is not appropriate to have a counselor onsite at that stage. Waiting until near the end of a shift may be prudent, however, it also is recommended that employees be allowed to sit and process news before driving or cycling, and offered a chance to talk amongst each other and exchange reactions.

Employees usually need time to process the news before talking to a qualified counselor. As someone who now consults corporations following a suicide, it is seldom in my experience that employees are ready to make use of a counselor brought in the day on which the news is being delivered. Some describe it as though they feel they are being pressured to "deal with" their grief reaction in that one session, then "move on and get back to work."

News of a sudden death, itself, is already difficult to process. News of a suicide doesn't quite compute in our brains in the same way. This is another reason why employers must exercise caution, and maintain preparedness for supporting the staff.

Desk space, lockers, and/or offices occupied by the deceased should be reassigned only after an appropriate amount of time has passed, and this will depend on the office culture or workplace environment. A bridge toll-taker's booth, for instance, would likely be immediately replaced by a colleague due to the job demands. An office cubicle used by the deceased may be a place for leaving flowers or tributes for up to several weeks after the death. Memorials or special tributes can be arranged, taking suggestions from colleagues who were close to the deceased.

Leaving an office space decorated for too long– several months or years (again, this is relative to the work environment) can become unhealthy if it starts to feel like a shrine immortalizing the decedent as a martyr. This can lead to a variety of dynamics, including a culture of fostering bitterness and resentment, low morale, diminished productivity, and could be damaging for survivors who may be at risk of suicide themselves.

Some employees may develop feelings of resentment towards an organization or management for increasing work loads, exacerbating stress levels contributing to the person's state of mind. Labeling a certain boss as a "tyrant," accusing him or her of being partially responsible for the person's overwhelming job-related stress and subsequent death, is not uncommon. Employees also may feel anger toward management for not intervening when an employee was in clear distress. For some, this may result in a sense of guilt over what possibly could have been done differently.

Some organizations will try to downplay the suicide; make reference that the cause of death was inconclusive; or suggest that the person's problems were not related to work. High profile companies may be very sensitive about bad publicity and nothing draws attention like the scandal of a taboo subject and suicide usually falls into this category. Coverups and misleading information can anger grieving families and loved ones and, in some cases, cause survivors to get stuck in a particular emotion of grief.

As weeks pass, survivors and affected employees will be in the early stages of processing their grief. Some may choose to return to work immediately, while others may need time away. Some who return to work days after a suicide may burn out after several weeks or even months, finding their emotions have caught up with them, and may require some time away to honor the process which will vary for each individual.

An inquest can trigger an emotional setback. Staff who had been functioning adequately may regress and need additional support and understanding.

If an employer can identify patterns of sick-absence, presenteeism, impaired functioning and poor performance, it becomes increasingly necessary to extend available support resources. This may include encouraging the employee/survivor to make use of the company's Employee Assistance Program (who usually offer short-term counseling), request an appointment with an Occupational Health consultant, or visit one's General Practitioner. Not everyone will want to pursue support, and that is each individual's personal decision.

In cases where there are colleagues of the deceased who, before the suicide, were already vulnerable and emotionally fragile either for work, family, or personal reasons, employers will need to be vigilant. The news of the suicide will most certainly exacerbate their stress levels. Managers are advised to make sure the employee is feeling supported and encouraged (not pressured) to take advantage of available support resources.

Some organizations may notice that months, even years after a work-related suicide, productivity declines and staff morale is low. Depending on the size of the company and how heavy the impact, recovery of the business may not always be possible. One suicide may seem relatively insignificant in the lifespan of a professional business; however the effects are far reaching and should not be underestimated. Employers who demonstrate genuine caring for their staff and remain dedicated to the ongoing promotion of employee health and wellbeing have a better chance of survival all around.

Whether it occurs within the workplace or outside of it, a death by suicide will impact members of the working population. It is hoped that this contribution will awaken everyone in a working environment to the impact and after-effects of suicide so that we can learn to understand the importance of offering the best support possible to all those affected.

****

CULTURAL DIMENSIONS

By John Peters, M.Suicidology

We have earlier in this book touched on the findings of Durkhiem that showed *at the time of his research* that the rates of suicide are influenced by the religious affiliation of the society under review. We also have seen that social changes within a country would seem to affect the rates of suicide and have seen how the gender and age differences can be very important.

This chapter looks at the way *suicide bereavement* can be influenced by our culture, both within the society as it is and also as it changes over time. The problem is that we have attitudes to the *intention* to suicide, to the *person* who has completed suicide, and to the *survivors* left behind after the event. So we could be very much opposed to the intention that our loved one has expressed to end their life. We can have mixed feelings about the person who has suicided and we can have sympathy for those left behind. However, life is never that simple and is complicated by our culture (and) community.

Our attitudes to suicide may be heavily influenced by the religion to which we adhere. In many cases, such as Christianity, Judaism, and Islam there have evolved scriptures which guide the adherent in his/her actions. Sometimes these guides made a great deal of sense at the time they were written, but one often questions their relevance today if literally applied. An example is that in the U.K. it used to be said that we should only eat pork during months that contained an "r" in the name. So we would not eat pork in May to August. This was of course because the pork was more likely to store badly in the warm weather and so cause illness. In a similar way, Judaism and Islam, originating in the Middle East, prohibited from the eating of pork in any month of the year. In the

U.K. today we will eat pork without fear of food poisoning due to our modern ways of food preservation. But Jewish and Muslim peoples will continue to reject pork in whichever climate they live, despite having adequate food preservation techniques. This must be an example of where a requirement of a culture at a specific time becomes enshrined in the religion and is firmly retained by all adherents.

However, many aspects of a religion can be subject to re-interpretation and an example is that despite the teaching of the Catholic Church against contraception, this religious law is ignored by the vast majority of its adherents.

In the case of suicide intention there is a fairly consistent view that we should make every effort to prevent suicide. The suicidal person will be of a mind that life is not worth living for one reason or another. A common cultural explanation is that for a person to end his own life prematurely can rob society, and particularly his family, of a valuable asset. The paradox of suicide can be seen in that in classical times there was honor in the nobleman "falling on his sword," but should a slave kill himself he was robbing his master, and society in general, of an asset.

The contradiction of the Abrahamic religions is that whilst, to a greater or lesser degree they have condemned suicide, there are many examples where suicide has been condoned and even encouraged. The biblical texts describe eight cases of suicide in the Old Testament and one in the New Testament, but none of them were condemned in the scriptures (Battin, 1994). Jews venerate the mass suicide of 960 Jews at Masada in the 1st Century A.D. and the suicide bombers of modern day Islam are viewed as martyrdom by some Islamists.

The critical scripture quote is the Sixth Commandment "*thou shall not kill*" (Exodus 20:13) and the interpretation of that phrase. St. Augustine is generally credited with the hardening of the church's position in viewing suicide as self-killing and so contrary to the Sixth Commandment, but the contradiction remained that it was acceptable for a country to kill others in time of war or to execute criminals in the name of the state.

Having declared suicide to be a sin, there was no way that the person could be punished for that sin in life, only in death. Penalties were imposed by the civil law as well as the canon law. There is a long history of the burial of suicides being outside the churchyard, without the services of the clergy, and at night. Even at the crossroads with a stake driven through the body as a warning to others. This arises from a longstanding belief that suicide was the ultimate unforgivable sin (by definition, repentance was not possible) and was first stated forcefully by St Augustine and reinforced by St Thomas Aquinas. The basis of this doctrine was that it was forbidden by scripture (thou shalt not kill) and was contrary to natural law (Parsons, 2010). But degrading a corpse was as futile as whipping a statue, observed Beccaria in 1764. Only God, he concluded, can punish suicide (Colt, 1987).

It seemed that society, not able to realistically punish the suicidee, then turned its attention to the estate of suicidee and his family. Goods were confiscated and often the surviving families were left in a state of penury. Voltaire called this practice "brigandage" adding, "His goods are given to the King, who almost always grants half of them to the leading lady of the Opera, the other half belongs by law to the Inland Revenue (Alvarez, 1972). The Christian and Jewish faiths do, however, have a "let out clause" which is to give the rites of burial to those who were "not of sound mind." As Parsons said "This useful pastoral route avoids seeming to condone suicide and both avoids the issue and introduces others. Who is to judge whether another person is 'of sound mind'? On what basis are the clergy given sufficient psychiatric skills and insight to determine this question– often with a person they hardly know?" Parsons pointed out that the Catholic Church in a new catechism stated: "We should not despair of the eternal salvation of persons who have taken their own lives. By ways known to him alone, God can provide the opportunity for salutary repentance. The Church prays for persons who have taken their own lives." In 1983, the Vatican repealed the canon law provision barring suicides from church funerals or burial in churchyards (Parsons, 2010, p. 3).

So we get to a key point of this chapter– how the family and friends are treated within their culture or how they perceive they are treated. It is certainly the way that their loved ones are treated that will influence how they feel. "I felt I was walking around with a brand on my head–'Suicide Survivor'" is a common reaction. In the 18th century survivors would conceal suicide to avoid the confiscation of property and the problems of burial but in the 19th-and early 20th-century families would conceal the truth of the suicide to avoid losing face, with fictitious explanations such as hunting accidents and heart attacks. Children were told the truth years later, if at all. There are some insurance companies in some countries that still do not pay out after a suicide or do not pay out until after the policy has been in place for two years. It is almost like society is taking out its punishment on the bereaved as they did centuries ago.

So families hid their grief and locked their guilt and anger inside themselves. They rarely sought professional advice unless these problems were uncovered by the professional when addressing a different issue. On many occasions blame is attached to the survivor, both from within and outside the family. The issues of stigma and shame continue, often more in the mind of the bereaved than in the mind of the wider society. This is an example of how our culture reaches back into the past and our attitudes can be influenced by our traditional culture even though our practices today may be very different.

However, our culture continues to evolve and today is changing at a fast rate due to the rapid transmission of ideas which have been accelerated by the development of the Internet, the media, and the increasing ability to travel and be exposed to other cultures. This process of acculturation can create confusion for many people who today may be simultaneously living in more than one culture. This can again give rise to the dichotomy of what the bereaved person knows rationally and what he/she feels emotionally.

We can easily recognize the difference in culture dependant on the racial or religious differences, but we should also be aware of the differences of gender, age, and in some cases the extent to which acculturation has taken place within communities that have transferred from one location to another. Most of us are sometimes painfully aware of the generation gap that we experience with our children or our parents. So we must be aware of such differences when we are supporting survivors. We should also be aware of the major differences between the feelings of members of a family. We very frequently hear, "Why can't he grieve like I do?" The answer is that we all grieve differently and this can be partly explained by our cultural differences.

References

Alvarez, A. (1972). *The Savage God.* New York: Random House.

Battin, M. (1993). Suicidology and the right to die. In A. Leenars (Ed.), *Suicidology: Essays in honor of Edwin Shneidman* (pp. 337-398). New Jersey: Jason Aronson.

Colt, G. H., (1987). The history of the suicide survivor: The mark of Cain. In E. J. Dunne, J. L. McIntosh, & K. Dunne-Maxim (Eds.), *Suicide and its Aftermath* (pp. 3-18). New York: Norton.

Parsons, M. (In press). *Suicide and the church.* Cambridge: Grove Books.

****

SETTING UP A SUPPORT GROUP

By John Peters, M.Suicidology

McMenamy, Jordan, and Mitchell (2008) have shown clearly that suicide survivors particularly value contact talking, one-to-one with another survivor and also highly value attendance of a specialist suicide grief support group. It also is notable that they found their approval is considerably higher than for a general grief support group or even for individual therapy.

We have previously suggested that there are three groups of survivors with varying needs.

- Those who cannot find help
- Those who do find and access help
- Those who do not wish to access help

I would suggest that the same applies to support group help and that we must cater for the wide range of survivors and their needs. The WHO/IASP (2008) in the booklet "How to start a survivor's group" describe the following advantages of such groups:

➢ Those bereaved by suicide often find it very difficult to admit that the death of the loved one was by suicide and often feel uncomfortable talking about the loss.

➢ Those bereaved by suicide therefore have less opportunity to talk about their grief than other bereaved people. A support group can assist greatly, as a lack of communication can delay the healing process.

➢ The coming together of those bereaved by suicide can provide the opportunity to be with other people who can really understand, because they have been through the same experience; to gain strength and understanding from the individuals within the group, but also to provide the same to others.

Perhaps the clearest evaluations are made by survivors themselves.

These are some comments made at one of our group meetings:

"The group gives me space in my busy life to grieve." –Melanie

"The only place I can go where people understand the depth of my grief." – Bill

"When I come to the group, I don't have to pretend to those present that I have stopped grieving." – Sue

"I feel so much better after attending the group because I have been able to release bottled up emotions." – Grace

A specialized suicide support group or a general support group?
The research of McMenamy et al. (2008) referred to above suggests that survivors significantly prefer specific support groups. Why should this be? I suggest the following reasons:

- Survivors may more readily accept the words of fellow survivors and then be willing to share experiences
- Survivors will recognize that suicide bereavement can take a long time
- Survivors will want to discuss the eternal question "*Why?*"
- Survivors may be consumed by the question "*What if?*"

Does it Have to be a specialize group?
My answer is that it does *not* have to be a specialized group. There will be many occasions when this is not possible for geographic reasons. Some survivors may prefer to join a group where they do not expect to feel the pain of being with others who have been bereaved by suicide.

What form of group?
There are a number of types of group, one case will be described in this chapter.

The options may be summarised in the following chart:

A **Closed Group** is where a group of survivors agree to meet for a set period of time. Further members do not join the group. This format has the advantage of the members getting to know each other and they often can see the progress made by other members even if they have difficulty in seeing their own progress.

An **Open Group (also called a drop-in group)** is one that invites survivors to join at any time. The door is open for them to join as well as to leave. The group is likely to include those recently bereaved as well as those who have been bereaved for some time. Here survivors who have been bereaved by some are able to offer support in an appropriate way based on his/her recent personal experiences. The choice to attend or not to attend is left entirely to the survivor who makes the decision if or when to return to the group. It may be that a survivor attends in the early days of bereavement, knows that the support is there, and decides to come more regularly at a later stage.

Peer Facilitation is a group led by survivors who have had some training in group leadership, although rarely have had formal external training. The important word is *facilitation* in that the facilitator is there to guide the members of the group to offer support to their each other without *directing* the work of the group. A major task of the facilitator will be to ensure that every member of the group has an equal opportunity to participate and that one member does not dominate the proceedings.

Professional Facilitation is obviously where a person with qualifications in bereavement support leads the group. Usually this means that the facilitator is not a survivor. Such a professional can bring a lot to the group and I work with such a friend who facilitates one of our groups. I would, however, suggest that a non-survivor who is interested in working with a group needs to spend some time as a visitor to a group to absorb the needs of survivors. Such a person may have to modify some of his or her previously held views and adapt procedures to the specific needs of suicide survivors.

Working Together (co-leaders) There will be many circumstances where a professional will work together with a survivor. This can well achieve the best of both worlds.

Starting a Group

The type of group and how it will be set up will depend on a range of local conditions, personal abilities, and requirements. My experience has been entirely with self-support voluntary groups that have been open groups and primarily peer led. Having been involved in the setting up of a number of groups I will describe what I have found has worked best for me, but accepting that there will be many other models that could be used:

- Investigate if there is an existing group for suicide bereavement close by. You will not do yourself a favour or the other group a favour if you are in the same regional area unless you work with different populations of survivors (like youth vs. adults).
- Try to visit a successful existing group, preferably at least several times.
- If possible, offer your services to an existing organisation. This will provide support and the possibility of training, website, telephone helpline, existing literature, etc. It also will mean that survivors will be more easily able to hear about your group.
- In either event you need to have help. Whoever you are, you can't enter into such a project on your own. You will need to have cover when you are on holiday or ill. You will certainly need emotional support when things get difficult and at any support group meeting you might have to deal with a difficult or troubled member and have someone else able to take over the members that remain in the room.
- A team of a minimum of three is to my mind essential to start a group. Not all of this group need regularly attend the meetings. For example, one person will need to act as treasurer and fundraiser. Another, perhaps a professional, may act as an adviser to the facilitators to help them with any problems that they may encounter.
- Do you/your team have the commitment to help others and sustain that commitment? Once a group is formed, the membership will need to know that the meetings will be regularly held. You cannot let people down when they are vulnerable due to their grief.
- Do you/your team have skills in facilitating a meeting, possibly under stressful conditions?

Please do not be put off by what might appear to be impossible constraints. We find that in almost every group we have people who desperately need help, understand that you have given up your time to help them, and can forgive minor shortcomings.

If you are working as part of a larger organisation, they will undoubtedly have procedures to ensure that you as an individual, those who come to you, and the organisation are all supported and protected against possible harm. This will certainly include the need to have basic insurance coverage.

First Steps

If you have made contact with two or three other people who are keen, to help I suggest the following plan of action:

1. Write to your local newspaper (letter to the editor) saying briefly that you are considering starting a support group for those who have been bereaved by suicide. You might mention that the group will be a local branch of a national charity if you have obtained agreement to do so. Ask anyone who wishes to hear more about the project to make telephone or email contact with you or another agreed contact.

2. Discuss with your personal contacts or local government offices the availability of a meeting room. The room will need to be:

- Available on a regular basis, like monthly.
- Large enough to hold perhaps up to twelve people with comfortable seating.
- Access to a toilet.
- Tea/coffee making facilities
- Ease of access for members. Can you park? Is there public transport? Is there disabled access?
- You may need to avoid controversial venues such as places of worship and health centres.
- Apart from early planning meetings, avoid using a member's home.

3. Discuss with your personal contacts, local charitable organisations, or local government offices the availability of funding. There is likely to be local funding available for new groups such as those offering support to survivors. Don't be put off by the need for funds, however, you will need to make the effort to find them.

4. You will need funds initially for:

- Hire of a meeting room.
- Cost of publicising the meetings– notices, postage etc.

5. You will need funds later for:
   - Cost of refreshments.
   - Cost of establishing a library of books specific to suicide bereavement.
   - Cost of establishing a specialist telephone line and its upkeep.
   - Cost of insurance.
   - Continuing cost of informing the public of what your group provides. Target undertakers/funeral homes, health centres, libraries, religious groups, therapists, and other support groups.

The First Meeting
Again you can write to your local paper to tell them that you are about to hold your first meeting and inform all those who have expressed an interest of the place and time of your meeting.

Some practical points:

- Arrange suitable notices on the access door(s).
- Have name tags/ labels available.
- Lay out a table with a selection of books and also with publicity material that members can take with them to distribute.
- Decide if you will have tea/coffee on arrival or perhaps after 60 or 90 minutes.
- I prefer to have the seats in a circle.
- The facilitator will welcome all and make any house notices.
- The facilitator will explain the intended format of the meeting and stress the absolute need for confidentiality.
- The facilitator will ask members to respect others and to give all members a chance to have a fair opportunity to contribute. He/she also will manage this need in the meeting.
- It will be made clear that everyone will be welcome to contribute; they will equally have the right not to explain their circumstances.
- You will need to have a list of those who attended, particularly in case a member had a problem, but do not have this list on public view as it should be confidential to the facilitator. I suggest you also have their telephone number. A member once took a set of car/ house keys by accident and we did not know her telephone number. It was chaos!
- Finally, remind everyone of the date of the next meeting.

Gauging Success

If you are running an open access group, there will undoubtedly be times when numbers fall and perhaps only the organisers turn up. *This is categorically not a failure.* You were there so that if someone turned up in need of help, that support was there. The very knowledge that the group meets, say every first Wednesday of the month, gives survivors the reassurance that there is help available *when they wish to access that help.*

Do not be disappointed if a survivor comes only once or a regular attendee stops coming. In each case the need may have been satisfied and you have done a good job. Some groups contact all those who have attended from time to time to remind them of the group, but if you do this include a delete slip to enable anyone who wishes to be taken off your list for further contact.

Why are groups healing?

Adina Wrobleski (1986) has described her experience of the groups she helped to set up in Minneapolis where she found that the most important benefit was the reassurance that it gave to survivors and the way that attending such groups breaks down the isolation that is imposed by the stigma of suicide. She stresses the value of self support groups as coming from the process of receiving help and the reassurance that one is not alone but also that the ability to reach out to help others, even in the midst of personal pain, can be very healing.

Working Together

Many professionals will recognise the need to set up a support group and my views above could be interpreted that the only way forward is by a peer-facilitated group as I have outlined above. This is not my intention. In many cases, the professional can support or initiate the survivor(s) to start a group. This support can be very valuable either as one of the facilitating team or by support behind the scenes. However, I stress the value that survivor volunteers:

- Can provide a passion for the organisation
- Can provide a unique perspective
- Can establish a rich empathy with fellow survivors
- Can provide a flexibility of availability– not tied to 9-to-5 office hours
- Often will have intensively studied the subject, sometimes to a deeper level than a qualified professional

References

McMenamy, J. M., Jordan J. R., & Mitchell, A. M. (2008). What do suicide survivors tell us they need? *Suicide and Life-Threatening Behavior*, 3, 375-389.

World Health Organization & International Association for Suicide Prevention. (2008). Preventing suicide: How to start a survivors' group. Geneva: Department of Mental Health and Substance Abuse, World Health Organization. Retrieved August 25, 2010 at *www.who.int/mental_health/prevention/suicide/resource_survivors.pdf*

Wrobleski, A. (1986). Aftermath of a suicide. *Bereavement Care*, 6(1), 2-3.

****

PROVIDING TELEPHONE HELPLINE SUPPORT

By John Peters, M.Suicidology

How can this support be provided?
There are a number of models of support that can be considered that are practiced in different countries and by different organizations that can be summarized as follows:

- Paid employees trained to provide support, usually with counseling qualifications.
- Volunteers who have experienced the trauma of suicide.

The organization of such support also may be provided in a variety of ways:

- From a central location where the telephone workers come to take the calls with the availability of support and resources.
- From the homes of the telephone workers who divert a common telephone access number to their home telephone.

We need to consider the nature of the support needed and likely frequency of calls in deciding the most appropriate form of service and also with regard to finance available to fund the project. Recent research by McMenamy, Jordan, and Mitchell (2008) shows clearly that survivors of suicide show the highest level of satisfaction by talking one-to-one with another suicide supporter.

It is perhaps an irony of suicide bereavement support that one of the biggest problems faced by those trying to help survivors is the relative infrequency of suicide in the U.K., where we average about fifteeen suicides a day. Even if all of these suicides resulted in calls to a support service, these calls could be handled by one worker (based on an average call of 30 minutes). Of course some survivors will call more than once and a suicide may well lead to more than one caller. My experience would suggest that most callers to our helpline will call just once and there only will be one call from the bereaved family.

But not all those affected by a suicide will need such help. We can define three basic groups of survivors as we discussed previously:

1. Those who cannot find help
2. Those who do find and access help
3. Those who do not wish to access help

My wife and daughters were originally in Group 1, but after about two years found help and moved into Group 2. I felt I could find my own solutions and put myself in Group 3.

For many survivors who do not feel able to attend a support group or visit a counselor, the opportunity to talk to a fellow survivor on the telephone can give a great deal of reassurance and knowledge that support is readily available. It also is reassuring that the survivor who makes the huge effort to make that telephone call can speak to a survivor and neither get a telephone answering machine nor have to make an appointment for days or weeks later.

An example of a Helpline in practice

Survivors of Bereavement by Suicide (UK) is a National Charity and covers the whole of the U.K. It was set up by Alice Middleton on April 16, 1991. Her brother had taken his life in 1983. She set up a peer support group in Hull and later Beverley, both in Yorkshire. Alice also held a conference for survivors in 1994 and from this start further support groups were set up across the United Kingdom.

In 2000, a National Telephone Helpline was established and has operated in substantially the way described below since its establishment. The Helpline is run by survivors for survivors. We do not offer a counseling service, but rather provide peer support by offering a listening ear and describing what services are available. We send each caller a booklet and further information written specifically for suicide bereavement.

It is a feature of suicide survivors that they are often on a quest to find answers: "Why did he do it?" "Will I ever recover from this despondency?" "What do I tell the children?" Survivors often will ask us if we have lost someone by suicide. They often feel greater empathy and willingness to talk if we reply in the affirmative. This raises an important question regarding peer support. How much of our own circumstances and our own views do we disclose? I do not feel that we can be talking parrots–merely repeating back what the survivor says. Rather we may use our own experience to help our caller but strictly draw the line at transferring our problems to the caller.

The Helpline is open from 9 a.m. to 9 p.m., every day of the year with the day divided into three, 4-hour sessions. Most volunteers will be on the Helpline for one session at a time whilst others will take longer sessions. It takes a total of about twenty volunteers to keep the Helpline manned. A volunteer works from home with a diversion system in place to direct the telephone line. This system has some disadvantages in that our volunteers, who are scattered across the country, sometimes feel somewhat isolated. We encourage them to talk to colleagues should they have a case they wish to discuss. It also means that we are not able to monitor the calls as we could if we were using a central call centre but so far in six years this has not proved to be a problem. It certainly means that the volunteer is able to spend most of the 4-hour slot at home doing other things, but available when a call comes through. The average Helpline session of four hours will involve perhaps three or four calls, varying in length from a few minutes to up to an hour and from a wide variety of types of callers–mostly from survivors themselves, but also from friends and professionals who are helping a survivor. All our volunteers report that although some calls can be stressful, they come off the telephone feeling that they have helped the caller and this gives them much satisfaction. This is reflected in the fact that we have few cases of burnout and most volunteers continue for a number of years.

It is most noticeable that we have calls from a wide range of time following the suicide. I had one call from a family friend of a suicide just three hours after the death and have had calls twenty, thirty, or forty years after the death. The calls from those who have been bereaved for a long time are often a result of children not being told about the suicide when a child and find out many years later that their parent had taken his or her life. The effect of bereavement can be just as profound in these cases. Other cases will be because the charity did not exist at the time of the bereavement or that they had not heard about us.

A significant problem for our very small charity is getting adequate publicity so that at least the gatekeepers such as GPs, counselors, and others in both the statutory as well as the voluntary sector are aware of our services. We are currently trying to address this issue by holding training sessions for healthcare professionals with the intention of creating a better understanding of the needs of suicide survivors as well as publicizing the services that we offer. We also see the need to improve the quality and distribution of specific material for statutory and voluntary agencies that may be in primary contact with the survivors.

The current volunteers for the Helpline have all been bereaved by suicide themselves and in many cases they will have availed themselves of our services and now wish to put something back. The volunteer will be interviewed and asked to attend a training session. There are such a variety of circumstances that can be brought to the volunteer that it is impossible to prepare for all eventualities. Rather we lay down basic guidelines and try to *empower* the volunteer to use his or her skills.

The training sessions are currently held twice a year and have a mixture of experienced and new volunteers so that valuable experiences can be shared. Our training is focused on the specific needs of suicide bereavement as we have had bad experiences where trainers from other fields of helpline work gave quite inappropriate advice for our circumstances. To some extent we are reviewing this policy, firstly by talking to other agencies and learning from their practice and seeing how we can improve our procedures.

Strengths and Limitations

One of the principal reasons for introducing the Helpline was to offer our services to all parts of the U.K. We currently take calls from all parts of Northern Ireland, Scotland, Wales, and England, though as previously mentioned we have much work to do to increase the knowledge of our services.

We find that many callers are now finding us on the Internet and one national number is very convenient to publicize. For many survivors, the opportunity to make a telephone call early or very early in their bereavement is most beneficial as this can break the isolation that most survivors feel following their loss. For many callers there is a benefit in anonymity and the opportunity to talk to new people who have not heard their story before but can listen and help from a different perspective.

The question of when a survivor should contact support services is frequently raised with some people voicing the view that a considerable period of time should elapse before the survivor makes this contact. The distinguished suicidologist, Adina Wrobleski, gave a very clear response. She quotes the experience of the five leaders of the Minneapolis/St Paul groups, all of whom are suicide survivors themselves. Their view was that one should be encouraged to seek help as soon as possible after the death. And that to suggest that it is in some way helpful for bereaved people to remain in their state of bewildered, painful helplessness ignores the pain of grief after suicide. (Wrobleski, 1986). I wholeheartedly endorse these sentiments. However it should be for the survivor to decide when he or she feel accessing support will help.

We have found that the Helpline is now a pivotal part of our work both as the way survivors make their initial contact with our charity but also to reassure them that they can call us at any time without having to book and wait. They will often call us at a time of anniversary or birthday.

Evaluation

The development of our Helpline has been largely based on what we feel the survivor needs, anecdotal feedback, and to some extent our intuition. However, we recognize that this is far from adequate and we have started to work with academic institutions in the evaluation of the work of both the Helpline and other support work. We see this as vitally important, both to ensure that we are delivering the best possible service as well as being able to show potential funding bodies that although we are a small voluntary charity we are able to provide an effective and specialised form.

Reference

McMenamy, J. M., Jordan J. R., & Mitchell A M. (2008). What do suicide survivors tell us they need? *Suicide and Life-Threatening Behavior*, 3, 375-389.

Wrobleski, A. (1986). Aftermath of a suicide. *Bereavement Care*, 6(1), 2-3.

****

STORIES BY THE BEREAVED

Mary's Story

A Love Story from Northern Ireland

A Note from John Peters: *Mary lost David through suicide in May of 2000 and contacted our Helpline about a month after David died. She used email to establish a conversation that I hope you will find encouraging in the way that such a conversation can be helpful as a means of talking to someone who can listen even from a far distance, obtain comfort, and make progress in the process of grieving.*

David and Mary had been going out for eight years, since Mary was fifteen, and had lived together for six years, but when David died she had no rights since they weren't married and David's mother was the person that the law determined should arrange the funeral. This was particularly hard for Mary as she felt cut off from her love at this time. This poignant account in Mary's own words as she felt at the time will give hope to many others who are bereaved by suicide. It also reflects the great courage that Mary has in facing the loss of her loved one and the variety of feelings that we all face when a loved one dies by suicide. However, David remains for her a support despite the heartache of his not being physically present. As she said, "He is an inspiration even if he is not here in body and mind; he is always here in soul and spirit."

Some readers might be surprised when they read in the later part of the chapter that Mary has found a new friend. Some may feel that their circumstances have been very different and that they have not been able to make new friendships in this way even years after their loss. Please do not be judgmental, we all proceed in our own way, but rather extend good wishes to all who find new friendships.

Hello (1) (First email 17th September 2000)

I don't know if it is unusual that it takes a while for everyone to get back to you. On many occasions I have felt like phoning, but I feel I am putting people out speaking to them. When I received your booklets I found them very helpful especially as they described exactly how I was feeling. I thought I was the only one feeling that way. Then I noticed you had an email address, which is great as I find as I talk in my head I can type it faster and the more I type the more I get into it and end up crying which sometimes I find can help as it exhausts me.

I am finding each day as a struggle. Today I was at the traffic lights on my way home and I looked to the jeep next to me and there was the CID man who came to confirm David was dead. He was also the one who brought me to the mortuary. He brought me there as we thought David's mum was not going to let me see him. I still find his death hard to accept. I also find it hard I didn't get to bring him home as I lived with him the last six years. When he would have a bad day I would phone his mum for help but she told me it was my problem and I had to deal with it. She also used to tell me to keep him away from the house when he was drinking. He wasn't all bad. Sometimes when I speak like this it sounds as if he was an ogre but he wasn't, he was more harm to himself than anyone else.

I find daily tasks very hard, dinner has got a bit easier but just to sit down and watch television and he is not there. I am sometimes glad that I didn't keep the house he died in, as I would probably find daily tasks harder. I really feel such a loss as if someone has taken a part of me away and I need it back. I went to our friend's 21st birthday party on Friday evening and stayed overnight but it just didn't feel the same. I didn't feel that I was doing something wrong it just felt as if he should have been there and it was very lonely. I told Janet, whose birthday it was, to keep his name on the invitation as she had already written it. I do feel relief as well as he is not here to put me through pain but I would have put up with that pain forever if I were given one more chance to keep him. He was my soul mate, my best friend, my everything. Before I received your pack I started to type out how I was feeling which I have attached. I still go to his grave everyday and I still can't believe it. I feel I shouldn't have to do it, not because he is there, but because he shouldn't be dead and I shouldn't have to go visit him at a grave but I should see him at home.

Thanks for listening. Well, I best go, thanks for your help.

Regards, Mary

WHERE AM I?

It's nearing three months and don't ever let anyone tell you it gets easier as it doesn't. If anything it feels as if it's worse and no one notices. I keep playing everything over in my head and it's not as if I wish to, it just happens and I want it to go away. I hear Jean's words over and over again in my head telling me he's dead. He can't be, this wasn't supposed to happen to David and he was invincible. Why? Feels like David used up his nine lives. Can anyone remember or am I just going through this on my own, can anyone hear me shouting, can anyone hear me crying?

I still go to the grave everyday and I haven't missed one day as yet. The bench has been put up in the graveyard today. I miss him so much, I feel so lonely, I miss the person who had the time to listen to me, who was always there for me, no one's there now. I can just about breathe on my own now but days I don't want to. Why can't I just go to sleep forever just peacefully? Just close my eyes some night and go forever. I don't want anyone to hurt but there's no one here. It's days like these that make David's escape seem like the best thing to do. I hope I never get as low as that but I wish I could go to sleep.

I had a dream that I went to heaven to ask why. He couldn't answer me and told me to go, as he was not allowed to tell me yet, as it was not my time and if I stayed any longer I would have to stay for good and he didn't want that. Why did I leave the dream; why didn't I stay? He said all he could tell me was that he loved me and he was happy. I do believe in my heart if he could have seen ahead he would not have done what he did and I do believe he did not mean to do what he did. I still see him in the coffin yet he shouldn't be there. Why couldn't that decision be left in my hands, as I would not have let him go; he was so precious? I'm scared I will forget, forget his face, forget his smile, forget the good times, is it normal to think you will forget? I don't want to forget, he was really special, he was my whole world. I'm scared I will especially forget the way he loved me and made me laugh, can you hear me cry now?

My footer message was, "Living here far away I am yours, Living there far away you are mine, Love is not in bodies, Just deep in our hearts and souls is where we are one."

Eternally yours, Mary

YOU NEVER KNOW

It's now nearing eight months since David died and, like I said before, there is a new person in my life. Sometimes I don't mention to anyone about the new person, as I am scared they will judge. He has already met two of David's sisters. It was okay as they both thought I should get on with my life, but one did think it was a bit soon. The reason they think it was soon as on August 27, 2000, my best friend told me I had to get out of the house and go out to a nightclub. She told me if I didn't go that she would come and get me. So my best friend and other friend headed out on this night. We went to a bar. First it was okay and I eventually settled. We had a drink in the bar and went on to the nightclub. After a while there I met my best friend from secondary school with another classmate. Along with my best friend was another friend and her cousin. So they joined our table. We were having a good night and danced the bit out. Then at one stage they went out to dance and she left her cousin with us at the table. I moved round to talk to him. At this stage I say to people who then laugh at me that I only moved round to chat that's what kind of person I am though they know that they only wind me up. We got up to dance and it went from there.

When we went to go home that night I was staying in my friend's house so we all walked to the taxi rank together. We got talking and I asked about previous relationships. He told me his last steady relationship was over two years ago and told me what happened. He then asked about mine. I proceeded to tell him that my relationship ended at the end of May this year and I am still wearing the engagement ring. I thought it best to tell him the truth from the beginning. He then asked what happened and I explained in little detail but the basics. Before we got into different taxis, we agreed to meet up the next day. When my best friend, my other friend, and I went back to her house we sat up and talked as she had family staying. It was good fun.

The next morning I awoke at 11.20 am. Lying in my sleeping bag next to me is my best friend and I shout to her, "What am I going to do?" as

I wasn't properly awake and I couldn't have driven. I got a taxi to where we were to meet at 12.00 pm. I was five minutes early. I was near McDonald's and needed coffee so I phoned a friend on my mobile but the battery was low. As I was waiting at McDonald's, his car drove past. I was like a child. I had butterflies in my stomach and I didn't know whether I was coming or going as I was so nervous. I went over to his car and we went for a drive to get something to eat and it's gone from there.

I am still going out with him and I honestly can't say or I won't say where it's going, only I am enjoying it while it lasts. I never felt guilty until Christmas, but it's not the guilt that I am going out with someone else. The guilt is there because I feel I have ruined one life and I don't want to ruin another. My new boyfriend is wonderful, but he will never replace David. But then I don't want anyone to. I am the kind of person who loves anyone and I do love him but in different ways. This I never thought I would find. We have talked about the past and he understands as much as anyone can expect him to. I am very lucky to have him, He is very understandable.

Regards, Mary

Dear John (A Final Thought),

Before I put in my last piece, I want to say that you have been really, really helpful and all the times I said I would ring and I didn't and I just kept emailing. I would have loved to have rung, but I find it easier to type it down as I think, but again, thank you, you have been a great support and guidance.

It's hard to know what to say. I read everything over again and it brought tears to my eyes because as time does pass you can't pass you can't remember being so down. But all my thoughts were true. The face and the happy times don't fade, not if you don't want them to. Mine's still there. Time heals slowly, time is still healing and like I said, probably always will. Christmas, birthdays get easier but it never goes away. No one ever forgets as silly things pop up so often. I still wish I could close my eyes in a dark silent room and everything goes away for a while. It's still there when you open your eyes, but you've had time to clear your thoughts. When someone takes his own life it puts so much into perspective. Life's too short for me. Like I said before, you do not know what is round the corner. Life's moving on, as I know David would have wanted and I'm being honest when I say I couldn't have done it without Barry. He has been a great support and so understanding and I love him more than he will ever know. He has been there to pick me up when I am down and many people would have turned and run but not him. But as for David he is at peace and looking after me well. I haven't gone back to the grave. We even moved to a new town last Christmas as after David died. A month later my parents broke up after twenty-six years marriage. So it hasn't been easy and there will be other things along the path to change your direction but you should never let that stop you. Carry on and hold your head up. If your head won't stay up, give it time, your smile will reappear.

And remember, "Love is not in bodies, just deep in our hearts and souls is where we are as one."

Kindest regards today and always, Mary

5/12/01

****

TRACY'S MESSAGE TO HER SON MARK

By Tracy McLeod

Tracy has chosen to write her story in the form of a conversation with her son. She first presented this at the Birmingham (U.K.) Support Day on May 1, 2010.

My beautiful son, Mark. You arrived in this world on 5th November 1988. It's true what they say you know, all the babies in the nursery were cute but none as cute as you. I was seventeen, had already survived two of what subsequently became six suicide attempts and, as much as I loved you, I couldn't give you what a child needs to grow and be happy. Gran and Papa stepped in, but you always knew I was mum. We always had fun together, you always knew when I left that I was coming back, you were never upset, you just seemed to understand.

You were such a happy little boy, the teenage years came and you put on weight and there was some bullying at school. You changed, you became wary of people, and somewhat reclusive. Not until you came to me at eighteen did we know to what extent the bullying had been. You were such a master of disguise, always hiding your pain. You came to live with me, we turned my one bedroom flat into bedsit land and really got to know each other. You were such an intelligent, intuitive, philosophical young man, knowledge beyond your years and your observations on life always blew me away. After what you had been through, you still didn't have a bad word for anyone else. You always made me laugh until I cried, tummy aching, laughing at me because I always thought I'd wet myself. We shared secrets, talked, analyzed, we weren't classic mother and son, there was even some role reversal, you often appeared to be the adult. You described us as peas, peas in a pod!

The opportunity came for you to spread your wings and move to Glasgow, to become independent, hopes of college and the future. On April 4 we kissed you goodbye, you were ten-feet tall and so full of excitement. We never knew that we'd never see you again, we never knew to stop you, we never knew that would we be the last time we would smell you, touch you, laugh with you...

On the 24th June, you posted your final tunes on Facebook, told the world that you where having your last coffee, your last cigarette, and said goodbye. With your passport and birth certificate in your pocket, the notes you had written and your favorite clothes on, you called an ambulance and told them you were going to throw yourself off your building and that's what you did. You didn't call them to stop you, just to come and collect you. At around eleven o'clock that day, I saw your Facebook post and called the police in Glasgow. At 12:00 my world was plunged into darkness; one phone call, you were dead! You, my gorgeous boy, noooooooooooo, not you!! I knew you'd been feeling low, had been prescribed some anti-depressants but you only waited five days, you never gave us a chance to help you, you never let me come to Glasgow when I wanted to, I respected your space but I shouldn't have.

Arriving at Gran and Papa's was surreal, we were all in shock, I collapsed the following day in physical pain, gut wrenching, heartbreaking pain. Two days later, I saw you, I hoped as I turned the corner that it wouldn't be you Mark, I so hoped but it was. You wouldn't wake up, lifeless, cold, where had my Marky Boy gone? I turned to valium and drink, I know Mark, what's new there? The following days were a blur of seeing family, your friends, collecting your things from the flat you shared. The reality of it all hadn't even began to sink in, valium helps you to defer the inevitable but seeing you in your coffin, knowing that I would never, ever see your face again was the most pain I will ever experience in my life. Your funeral was horrendous, I didn't want them to take you, there was no comfort for me that you were with God and Pops in heaven. You hadn't been ill, you'd never talked of death. I had been submerged into a place I could not understand, feelings and thoughts I couldn't accept, I wanted to stay with you, how could I let them take you away from me Mark, you were mine?

I ran away for a while after that, into a delusional world of denial and shock. I didn't really return to my life for about three weeks then the real world crashed in on me. I had to learn to live without you. All of the color left my world, everything became shades of black and grey. The physical pain was never ending, the tears never stopped flowing, I was walking around Solihull in a daze. I could hear the world around me, but felt like I was in a bubble, invisible, the clock ticked on, the world still turned, and I felt no part of it. I wanted to scream out, STOP, just stop, he's dead and I wish I was, too!! I wanted to be with you, not here with this crushing pain, there was no future without you.

The living hell became worse when the questions started, Mark, when did you decide, why didn't you call me, what were you thinking when you were standing on that ledge, were you upset, did you die straight away, how long did they leave you lying on the pavement, had I let you down, how could I not have known, how could I have let you die?? Never ending whys, never any answers but going mad with the need for them. Guilt crucifying me, nightmares, crying myself to sleep, not wanting to get up and start another day without you. Time, a healer, hey Mark, all I could see was years ahead of me living in this dark, excruciating hell!! Hindsight brought with it even more crippling pain, your extreme weight loss, were you bulimic? I know your eating pattern was bizarre, that period of depression you had, your crazy sleep deprivation so you wouldn't sleep in for work, the recreational drugs you started taking in Glasgow, a dangerous combination! Damned hindsight, what good was it to me now, I couldn't save you!!!!! All it did was torture me.

Your twenty-first birthday was celebrated, Gran had a party, we went through the motions and everyone cried and cried. Nothing had changed, I was back at work, pretending that life had to go on, seeing people but only being with them in body, no connection to anyone, I didn't care anymore. I often got mindlessly drunk, took to bed for days, nothing changed. Christmas came and I descended into a place even darker, I decided to join you. I started to make my plans, life was never going to be worth living without you. I thought of Gran, Tanya, and the kids, Rhona, how could they survive us both leaving, how could I double their pain? I cried out for help and that help came. Friends saved me, medical help came in the form of talking, medication for my own depression, and somehow I've turned a corner. I understand the feeling of desiring death, I'm not angry that you left, I gain comfort from your release from pain. I realized that I was never going to get you back, that you were safe from all that scared you, how could I expect that you should stay and feel that, my own pain at your absence cannot match the pain that drove you to throw yourself from that building.

Mark, I have to go on and find a future, to celebrate your life, to try and enjoy what I can. I can now say that there are still moments of despair but not every waking minute of every day, the sadness is not as crushing and heavy as it was, colour has returned to my world, albeit very slowly, but it is there. I focus on how grateful I am for the time we had, the light you shone in my world, the truly beautiful man you were, the peace you now have.

I met a couple who'd just lost their son. I recognized their raw pain, I'd heard myself say all of things they had, I realized how far along this road I'd come, to comfort them gave me some comfort, too, I wasn't alone! I cried hearing their story, I was grateful for small mercies, no inquest, not being the one that found you, you made it so much easier for us, even at the end you thought of everything and spared us as much as you could. I wish that you could have seen what the world could offer you because it was a much better place with you in it. I understand Baby Sprout, I'm trying to let go of the crippling guilt I feel, I know you told me that I did the right thing, I know the first line of your note told me it wasn't my fault, I know that you loved me but that's hard to accept now that you've left. I hope you never felt rejected, I hope you are happy, I love you, Sprout, I burst with pride when I talk of you and I will miss your light forever.

I have fallen in love with a wonderful man, Sam. I never thought my heart could love again but I know you would want that, I know you'd be so cross if I gave up, I will make you proud of me. It keeps me going to think that maybe you can see and maybe you're smiling. I've fallen in love with a cat, too, her name is Penny. We always wanted a cat didn't we? I'm going to live with Sam and Penny, I'm going to build a future, without your physical presence, but with you in my heart.

Thank you for all that you were, all that you still are in my memories, thank you for your love, I will always have your love. THANK YOU!!!

Remember our little song, 'Me love you, yes me do and me know that you love me, too!'

****

THE IMPACT OF THE BEHAVIOR AND PRACTICE OF OTHERS ON THE GRIEVING PROCESS OF FAMILIES BEREAVED BY SUICIDE

By Michelle Flood, D.Ed Psych

This chapter documents findings from a case study conducted to explore the impact of bereavement by suicide on family life. An in-depth interview was conducted with a woman, named Laura for the purpose of this chapter, who, as an adult, lost her brother to suicide. Her account offered an insight into how the behavior and practice of others served to either exacerbate or ameliorate the bereavement experience for her and her family. Laura's story is relevant to medics, police personnel, and those involved in the judicial system, as well as members of any community to which survivors belong. The chapter concludes with recommendations for those coming in contact with survivors so that they can optimize their support role.

Professionals

First Responders. First responders to the scene of a suicide death have a vital role to play in the initial and long lasting impact of the trauma on suicide survivors. Laura discussed the practices of the first responders to the scene of her brother's suicide; in particular the General Practitioner (GP) and the police force.

Medics. Medics have the difficult task of arriving to the scene of a suicide and pronouncing the death of a family's loved one. If this is not done in a sensitive manner, it can intensify the horrendous situation. Laura described how the delay in the doctor arriving to the scene exacerbated the experience for her and her family:

"...but we waited two and a half hours ... I just think 'You know, how dare you, all you had to do was come out and pronounce him dead.'"

What may seem like a routine task for some medics is a moment that will force family members to re-evaluate their life forever. The traumatizing experience of the pragmatic approach of the doctor was illustrated by Laura:

"My brother goes 'doctor he's alive' and the doctor turned and 'it's just like trapped air.'"

Police. The arrival of the police in a squad car and full uniform seemed like an unnecessary, bureaucratic procedure that clinically intruded on a horrifying, but intensely personal event for family members:

"...they came back in full uniform with the hats and everything, a car outside, a squad car outside with a blue light on the top of it...it's not a crime scene."

Laura acknowledged that their presence was required but suggested that they be allowed to arrive in plain clothes and an unmarked car to reduce the distress caused.

Laura also was concerned that appropriate support or training was not provided for members of the police who have to deal with a suicide death.

Psychological Support

A lack of understanding among professionals who provide psychological support to suicide survivors has been cited in the literature (Grad, Clark, Dyregrov, & Andriessen, 2004). This was reiterated by Laura, who found the experience of counselling not only unhelpful but also to have an iatrogenic effect on her grieving process:

"... she actually set me back again because I was doing ok, and she just, she just annoyed me and she just, 'ah,' I just cried the whole back, I was so sorry that I ever went up near her."

When Laura sought professional support she had to wait fifteen months before such support was available, only to feel the counselor showed a complete lack of understanding and sensitivity to her and her experience. This was demonstrated through the counselor's body language and verbal comments. Laura believed that an understanding of suicide bereavement could only be acquired through personal bereavement either by suicide or another death.

Laura also highlighted a lack of support for children. This deficit was evident at various points in the children' development and Laura implied that the young family members were never able to truly process their grief:

"He took everything in, yeah, took everything in, and didn't know how to release it all back out again, and we did worry about him for a long time and I still do. He's very quiet. He's seventeen now."

Laura said that her main source of support was talking to and helping other suicide survivors. She identified becoming involved in a support group for survivors as imperative to her grief resolution:

"I find talking, probably the best thing I ever done was to get involved with [Suicide Bereavement Support Group], and to go out helping other bereaved families."

This has also been reported by survivors in existing research (McMenamy, Jordan, & Mitchell, 2008).

Inquests

The impact of the inquest procedure following a suicide death on surviving family members has been researched (Barraclough & Shepherd, 1977; Biddle, 2003). Despite the 26-year gap between these studies, their findings were ominously similar; the inquest procedure exacerbated the grieving process for suicide survivors through its perceived lack of sensitivity to the survivors' needs and its destructive impact on the process of sensemaking for the survivors. Laura also described her negative experience of the inquest procedure. Laura explained the traumatic experience of attending the inquest, being forced to sit through other cases, and having to listen to intimate and painful details of her brother's death:

"I just thought it was absolutely horrific that day to be sitting there, for what to watch people, to listen to other people's stories that were so personal."

The inquest did not answer any questions or provide the family with any further information that may contribute to their understanding of the death:

"Like I was up there thinking 'Was there drugs in the system? Was there drink? What were we going to be told? We were told that his neck was broke, sure we already knew once he was cut down that his neck was broke."

Laura described being completely unprepared for the inquest having received no information regarding what the day would entail and being taken aback by the presence of the jury. Although not particularly relevant to her experience, Laura discussed the experience of others who had to wait up to two years for the inquest to take place; a delay that served to postpone grief resolution:

"Some people have waited over two years which is huge because it's there, it's in the back of your mind, that you have to go through this, not knowing."

Media

Media reports of intimate details of the death, and family members' reactions to both the death and the inquest experience were found to be insensitive and unnecessary:

"Our story was splattered all over the newspaper...it's nobody's business."

It was difficult to see the benefit of these reports; rather they resulted in yet further pain for the surviving family members.

The Community

Laura commented on the practical and emotional support provided by friends, neighbors, and the wider community as well as her experience of stigma.

Practical Support

Laura and her family valued practical support from their neighbors in the aftermath of the death:

"...people came with food, people came with stews, the butchers came with meat ... one cooked beef, one cooked lamb, one cooked chicken, one cooked everything, and they all brought it to the house, one done veg, one done spuds, and everything... so neighburs and friends yeah, very, very important."

"Ah if they could do anything for us, for his anniversary you know, even them going to cut the grass on the, on the, on the grave."

This demonstrated solidarity and allowed family members to focus on their grief rather than concerning themselves with everyday tasks.

Emotional Support

The emotional support provided by friends and neighbors was also appreciated. Friends and neighbors calling to talk with family members and to listen to their feelings and stories were identified as helpful. However, Laura also reported that at times the family wanted to be left alone in their grief:

"But then sometimes you love to be on your own."

It seemed that a balance between letting family members know that support was available and allowing them time and space to grieve was important.

Laura also implied that as time moved on, people began to get on with their lives, leaving the family to grieve alone:

"What we found was after the months Mind Mass (a Mass said a month after the person died), that's when everything just [pause] and that's when you need people to come in and say, 'hey we haven't forgotten.' I do say 'we're like survivors of suicide.' Anyone that's bereaved of suicide, we're survivors; we just have to keep going on. We're also the forgotten grievers because it's like as soon as, as soon as the months mind goes and maybe it's because people maybe want to leave you alone for a while; you have to grieve, but at the same time it's when my mum and dad needed someone."

This experience has been reported by other survivors (Begley & Quayle, 2007; Lindqvist, Johansson, & Karlsson, 2008).

Stigma

Laura described the pain of experiencing stigma. She spoke of how people actively avoided her:

"...the two women coming as far as the door and seeing me and just turning and walking away again and it was just, my heart just sank into my tummy."

She understood that this was in part due to people's lack of understanding as to how to approach survivors:

"They just didn't know what to say to you. They didn't know. If they said something and I got upset they'd be blaming themselves."

She recommended that people be honest about their lack of understanding, but open about their desire to help:

"Neighbors, they just came in, they just went, 'No, we don't, we haven't a clue what you're going through, but if you want to talk about it, you know, we're there.'"

Laura also spoke about the unacceptable use of the term *committed suicide*. She reported hearing its use among professionals and members of the community and told of how it contributed to the pain of surviving members. Suicide is no longer considered a crime but the continuous use of the word commit means the criminal connotations are retained, causing much distress for suicide survivors.

Conclusion

The aim of this chapter was to highlight areas for consideration by professionals and members of the community when interacting with suicide survivors. Findings were based on the story of a woman who had been bereaved by the suicide death of her brother and were related to existing findings in the literature. The points raised are summed in the following recommendations:

- Medics must react swiftly and sensitively to the notification of a death by suspected suicide. The delicate act of the confirmation of death should be done in a way that would minimize the trauma for family members.
- Consideration should be given to the possibility of police workers arriving in plain clothes and unmarked cars to the scene of a suicide death and when collecting statements at a later stage.
- Sufficient training and support for police should be provided; this should be based on accounts from suicide survivors as reported in the literature.
- Professionals designing support for suicide survivors should ensure that they develop an understanding of the grieving process as told by the survivors themselves.
- Suicide survivors value support from others who have shared the experience of suicide bereavement.
- Support for vulnerable groups, including children, should be made more available.
- There is a need for the inquest procedure to be reassessed and revised in order to minimize the distress it causes for suicide survivors.
- The media should develop a greater understanding of the potential pain reports can trigger for suicide survivors and refrain from causing unnecessary distress for them.
- Friends, neighbors, and the wider community can assist family members in their grief by:

- providing practical support
- letting the family know that they are available and being honest about their concerns about saying or doing anything that would exacerbate the grief
- The word *commit* should be removed from the language of suicide. The phrase *commit suicide* should be replaced by terms such as *completed suicide*, *died by suicide*, or *took his/her own life*

References

Barraclough, B. M., & Shepherd, D. M. (1977). The immediate and enduring effects of the inquest on relatives of suicide. *British Journal of Psychology*, 131, 400-404.

Begley, M., & Quayle, E. (2007). The lived experience of adults bereaved by suicide. *Crisis*, 28(1), 26-34.

Biddle, L. (2003). Public hazards or private tragedies? An exploratory study of the effect of coroners' procedures on those bereaved by suicide. *Social Science and Medicine*, 56, 1033-1045.

Grad, O.T., Clark, S., Dyregrov, K., & Andriessen, K. (2004). What helps and what hinders the process of surviving the suicide of somebody close? Crisis, 25(3), 134-139.

Lindqvist, P., Johansson, L., & Karlsson (2009). In the aftermath of teenage suicide: A qualitative study of the psychosocial consequences of the surviving family members. *BMC Psychiatry*, 26(8). Retrieved 18 January, 2010 from http://www.biomedcentral.com/1471-244X/8/26.

McMenamy, J. M., Jordan, J. R., & Mitchell, A. M. (2008). What do suicide survivors tell us they need? Results of a pilot study. *Suicide and Life-Threatening Behavior*, 38, 375-389.

****

STANDBY: A PROACTIVE POSTVENTION RESPONSE SERVICE IN AUSTRALIA

By Jill Fisher, M.Suicidology, (Australia)

"Mahatma Ghandi believed that an ideal community is one that resembles the human body where, whilst different parts of the body may have different functions, in a time of crisis the whole body galvanizes to deal with an injury. Ghandi believed an ideal community would emulate this response of the human body and in a time of crisis come to the aid of those in need" (Ghandi, 1998).

Bereavement through suicide has considerable emotional, social, and economic impacts which have only recently gained recognition by the broader community. With more than 30,000 directly experiencing a significant loss through suicide each year in Australia alone, the imperative of providing best practice local bereavement support continues to underpin the work of StandBy across Australia.

Suicide is a time of immense crisis and the tragedy of suicide loss creates trauma and turbulence deeply affecting an entire community (Paul, 1995). Freud noted that the greater the degree of trauma, the greater the stress. This is especially true for suicide since there is almost no other death in society for which there is a higher social (and often personal dynamic) stigma for the survivors (Leenaars, 2001). Culturally, also, the sense of rejection experienced by suicide bereaved in a kinship society or close-knit community can be even more profound as rejection implies not only immediate familial relationships but also a rejection of the entire community, its culture and its future (Tatz, 1999). Without appropriate support and linkage, individuals can then feel further isolated in their grief and become at risk themselves of engaging in suicidal ideation and behaviour (Krysinska, 2003). Edwin Shneidman's definition of psychache (Maris, Berman, & Silverman 2000), which refers to hurt, anguish, and aching pain in the psyche, also can describe the feelings of those exposed to trauma such as suicide. Whilst for many reasons, communities may not take the first initiative to respond, survivors, due to their traumatic experience and its effects, are themselves unable to ask for help or articulate their need (Dyregrov, 2002).

However, within communities those social relations and structures which can produce such traumatic reaction and pain also contain within them the capacity for response and the ability, in a time of crisis, if comprehensively managed and coordinated, to effectively come to the aid of those in need. A well coordinated, sustainable, and continuous postvention service is the foundation of the Standby Response Service.

The origins and growth of StandBy

StandBy is a community-based active "early intervention" postvention program that provides a 24-hour coordinated crisis response to assist families, friends, and associates who have been bereaved by suicide. Standby is managed by United Synergies a not-for-profit organisation committed to making a difference in the lives of others. United Synergies is based in Tewantin, Queensland.

The Sunshine Coast and Cooloola region comprises diverse communities and includes rural residents in the isolated hinterland areas through to the popular coastal areas. The area is well known for its tourism and hospitality industries yet, despite the beautiful environment and glossy image, the region experiences relatively high rates of suicide in several localities. Several years ago, a suicide triggered the deaths of several other members of the same family. This incident, and other traumatic losses, severely impacted the resilience of a small Australian community to cope in an environment where infrastructure had not kept pace with rapid growth. Following an extensive evaluation by a local community health service, the StandBy Response Service was established in 2002.

In 2006, with the assistance of the Australian Government Department of Health and Ageing, a trial project was commenced to replicate the program in three additional communities– Cairns, Canberra, and North Brisbane. In 2009, further expansion of the program occurred, with the establishment of services in Western Australia and Tasmania. The service now operates in nine locations across Australia: the Sunshine and Cooloola Coasts, QLD; Cairns & Far North Queensland, QLD; North Brisbane, QLD; Canberra and the ACT; the Pilbara region, WA; the East

& West Kimberley, WA; Southern Tasmania; and North/North Western Tasmania auspiced by a number of local organisations and managed nationally by United Synergies. The program continues to receive considerable national and international exposure generating enquiries from other communities about StandBy and expanding StandBy for LiFE training programs in response to community need.

StandBy continues to be embraced by communities across Australia and welcomed as a viable and sustainable local initiative which aims to reduce adverse health outcomes and further suicidality for people bereaved by suicide.

The StandBy model of bereavement care

The StandBy Response Service is a community-based postvention model that builds cooperative networks and partnerships within the community to facilitate more effective and efficient response to suicide incidents. In addition, the service provides immediate support and referral services, twenty-four hours a day, seven days a week, for anyone bereaved by suicide, no matter when or where the suicide occurred, via a locally based and staffed 24-hour crisis response telephone number. From there, people bereaved by suicide can receive face-to-face outreach service provided by a skilled crisis response team and/or referral to appropriate support services matched to their needs, coordinated by a highly-qualified program coordinator. In a situation of immediate suicide bereavement, referrals are made by emergency response services whose vehicles currently carry refrigerator magnets displaying the 24-hour hotline telephone contact or via referral from other community agencies when previous bereavement by suicide has become a significant issue for survivors. The service also supports emergency and community services providers who respond to suicide events and help to build understanding to cope with suicide loss at the scene and afterwards.

Furthermore, StandBy also has the capacity to assist schools, workplaces, and community groups to manage a suicide incident, providing support ranging from information and guidance through to workshops, training, and crisis management. StandBy's postvention services are provided always and only by invitation from the bereaved. Experience with Standby indicates many bereaved people prefer to have opportunity to choose the time and venue (usually within their home) for direct face-to-face support and appreciate this respectful practice approach.

Within each community, the program is guided by a steering committee, consisting of a range of representatives from across the local area, including police officers, ambulance staff, funeral directors, coronial staff, counsellors, cultural representatives, and bereaved people. The steering committee works with the StandBy coordinator and staff to identify current community issues, potential partnerships, and existing service gaps. StandBy also establishes formal partnerships, arrangements, and memorandums of understanding with other local services, which enables referrals between StandBy and other agencies.

Community strength and knowledge also is enhanced via the StandBy for LiFE Pathways to Care Community Workshops including the "Crossing the River" Suicide Bereavement Training. Key informants such as suicide survivors, police, ambulance, and other first responders assist in delivery of community training also which includes significant involvement by representatives from local Aboriginal and Torres Strait Islander communities. Following these local training events, a referral pathway flow chart identifying plan participants is formulated for each locality and is suitable for self-referral by clients or as an adjunct to the provision of a coordinated community response. Now an internally developed database, the document provides extensive information about more than several hundred local and national community groups, services, or individuals able to provide support to bereaved. All nominated agencies have been sensitized to the issues faced by suicide survivors and have made formal commitments to service provision as part of the pathway process.

StandBy also provides media management and liaison in the wake of suicide within the terms of pre-determined agreements with community partners as guided by the World Health Organization and Australian Government Mindframe principles. The StandBy model enables provincial areas to implement effective response plans built on increased knowledge of suicide bereavement gained via community education and integrated training approaches, then develops and maintains an integrated range of support services, including survivor groups, as well as a database to assist future research. By mobilizing resources and encouraging active participation by a wide range of existing networks and peak regional bodies as well as agencies such as police, ambulance, courts, community groups and health services, this model, in evaluation, effectively reduced the difficulties experienced by bereaved people in accessing support and demonstrated its capacity to reduce suicidality for people bereaved by suicide.

"I am glad about this thing called StandBy that has come to our town."

The StandBy journey has been encouraging, exciting and humbling as StandBy acknowledges the privilege of being invited into the lives of individuals and communities in a time of loss. However the moments that remain at the heart of StandBy are the stories which tell the true journey of StandBy:

The first immediate response undertaken by Southern Tasmania StandBy, a call that came through from the police during an early team training session. StandBy responded to a grief stricken family. Then when readying to leave, they discovered neighbors who had found the person so the team just sat down all over again next door and extended such important and vital support...

The Brisbane StandBy team who when reaching out to a family of African refugees whilst providing support, also absorbed knowledge from them about their mourning needs then translated this knowledge to action and achieved significant changes with usual government accommodation services that made their pain "just a little more bearable"...

Two young girls in the Pilbara whose grief was so entangling that they could not even imagine a future yet StandBy sat with them through their pain and began in a gentle way to open the door of their suffering just enough to let in a little hope...

The outreach by the West Kimberley StandBy to a local community at a time of several devastating losses when StandBy critically coordinated all services together in a way acknowledged by all participants as vital and groundbreaking...whilst still offering individual support to a community much loved by members of the StandBy team...

The support from the Canberra StandBy service to a family which provided such succor and strength that the StandBy team was written about with deep gratitude as "angels in the darkness"....

The support to a grieving partner provided by the North/NW Tasmania StandBy service when complicated family arrangements and financial challenges meant funeral plans became yet another painful experience and disenfranchised grief of a non-recognized partner was met by StandBy support...

The family in North Queensland who did not miss their son's funeral in far-off Melbourne because StandBy was there in their time of need...

The family who attended the Sunshine & Cooloola Coasts Remembrance event having after much hesitation, finally been supported by StandBy in the loss of a beloved nephew just a few months earlier and then sending a letter of such gratitude explaining that when freeing one of the white doves during the ceremony as the bird rose to the sky some of their pain, too, lifted and they were able for the first time to recall times of joy amongst their sorrow...

And especially the bereaved mum in the very remote town of Kununurra Western Australia who humbled all with her story of loss and lack of support prior to StandBy then humbled all again with her simple statement, "I am glad about this thing called StandBy that has come to our town" and made many kilometers of roads, heat, dust cyclones, cold, fog, and sunshine worthwhile for the StandBy service...

We, too, are "glad about this thing called StandBy" that has come to so many places across Australia and proactively responded to the needs of those traveling the long and winding road of suicide loss.

References

Dyregrov, K. (2002). Assistance from local authorities versus survivors' needs for support after suicide. *Death Studies, 26*, 647-668.

Ghandi, A. (1998). Lessons from Sevagram Ashram. In F. Hesselbein, M. Goldsmith, R. Beckhard, & R. Schubert (Eds.), *The community of the future* (pp. 83-90). San Francisco: Jossey-Bass.

Krysinksa, K. E. (2003). Loss by suicide: A risk factor for suicidal behavior. *Journal of Psychosocial Nursing & Mental Health Services, 41*(7), 34-41.

Leenaars, A. (2001). Suicide prevention in schools: Resources for the millennium. In D. Lester (Ed.), *Suicide prevention: Resources for the millennium* (pp. 213-235). Philadelphia: Brunner-Routledge.

Maris, R., Berman, A., & Silverman, M. (2000). The theoretical component. In R. Maris, A. Berman, & M. Silverman (Eds.), *Comprehensive textbook of suicidology* (pp. 26-61). New York: Guilford.

Paul, P. (1995). The development process of a community postvention protocol. In B. Mishara (Ed.), *The impact of suicide* (pp. 64-72). New York: Springer.

Tatz, C. (1999). *Aboriginal suicide Is different Aboriginal suicide in New South Wales, the Australian Capital Territory and New Zealand: Towards a model of explanation and alleviation.* A Report to the Criminology Research Council on CRC Project 25/96-7. Sydney: Centre for Comparative Genocide Studies Macquarie University.

****

WORKING CREATIVELY WITH BEREAVED CHILDREN

By Pam Dean, M.Ed. Counselling, MBACP

Children will tell you of their bruised and
broken knees but have no words
for their bruised and broken hearts.

How can we help young people voice the many emotions, thoughts, and concerns they have following bereavement by suicide? A death that can, at the time, and during ensuing months, seem like an overwhelming life event. The focus of this chapter is to share some creative ways young people have engaged with that have helped them to express and share their pain and loss. My hope is that the sharing of these experiences will be of help to others also supporting young people.

I use the term "creative" in its broadest sense, encompassing not only art materials but play dough (other malleable materials), a variety of boxes, puppets, soft cushions, buttons, shells, stones, fabric scraps, glitter, etc.

Why is art helpful when working with young people?
Art is a natural language for most children and adolescents, providing the child with a way of expressing and communicating their experiences and feelings as well as their practical everyday worries. Malchiodo (2003) believes art can be a form of expression that enables children to express their trauma, distress and loss while Gross and Haynes (1998) note that art expression may:

- Help to reduce the child or young person's anxiety thereby helping them feel more at ease when working with a therapist or other professional.
- Be the means by which they give shape and structure to their

stories.

- Provide an opportunity for the young person to share more of their experience through a medium other than words.

When working with children it's important not to make assumptions about content and meaning. Their art and creative expressions have to be viewed with openness to a variety of meanings (Malchiodi, 2003). I therefore work from a person-centered approach, an approach that is non-directive and non-interpretative of the child or young person's work. I trust and accept that the child knows what he or she needs to do and that they will do so at a time and at a pace that is right for them.

When working with grieving children the therapist or helper will need to have an understanding of the numerous issues involving loss and grief.

Contracting

When beginning work with a child, I go through the practicalities:

- How long each session will last.
- The number of sessions.
- Confidentiality, its meaning, its limits.
- What happens to their work– I provide a cardboard box and after each session work is put in this for safe keeping. When our work together comes to an end the child decides whether or not he/she will take their box home.

Providing a cardboard box in which a young person can put his/her work keeps it confidential and safe. I let the child decorate his/her box in any way her/she chooses to make it personal. Although this activity often takes up a whole session, it can become a shared venture, which helps 'break the ice.'

Beginning Work

One of the first tasks when working with children is to build a trusting relationship, the foundation of the therapeutic process and can, in itself, be powerfully therapeutic. To do this I need to enter the child's world, listening to and staying with what interests the child. An example of this is work with nine-year-old Tom.

When Tom first arrived he was withdrawn and angry, didn't want to look at me, and had no interest in any of the play or art items in the room. I let him know that was okay, but I wondered how we could get to know each other? A shrug and for the rest of the session Tom became deeply interested in studying his 'broken' mobile phone!

He began the next session by drawing a keypad on a large piece of paper complete with 'send' button. He then 'wrote' his text, pressed 'send' and turned the paper to face me to 'text' back. He didn't talk throughout this process. I replied, pressing the 'send' button' and Tom replied back. Paper 'texting' became our form of communication for several weeks and was the beginning of our relationship.

From his 'texts' I learned he was mad about cricket and wanted to be a wicket keeper. This led us to throwing a cushion at each other, to test 'wicket keeping skills,' making each throw more difficult than the last. This, too, went on for several weeks, until Tom changed the rules. The aim was now to throw lots of cushions to each other to see how many each could hold while catching another cushion at the same time. He found this fun, especially winning. And then, halfway through one game, he suddenly and briefly spoke of his brother's death.

At our next cushion throwing session Tom again suddenly stopped and spoke about his brother. Slowly a new pattern emerged of throwing cushions, talking, and then using the cushions as a release for emotions. They could be safely thrown, punched, or snuggled into when the tears came. It was during one of our 'talking times' that Tom told me that the broken mobile phone he brought to all our sessions, had belonged to his brother. It was a painful moment of acceptance of his loss when Tom acknowledged that while he wanted his brother to text him he now knew he couldn't.

Staying with Tom, entering into his world through his ideas and games gave him control and enabled him to share his misunderstandings, his grief and anger over his 19-year-old brother's death by suicide.

Working with Shells, Buttons and Stones

Seeing their world through their eyes.

Why introduce this way of working?

The use of external objects can be helpful for a child or young person as:

- Talking about what is on the paper is easier than talking directly to someone.

- The image and the paper holding it provide containment for difficult issues and feelings.
- They voice their perception of how others are thinking and feeling.
- It enables them to gain a different perspective on their world.
- It can help with exploring attachment and loss.
- They can show changes they would like to see or make which can then be explored.

For the therapist, the use of external objects gives:

- Clarity of a complex or close-knit family structure.
- Understanding of the child's perceived or real world.

A variety of shells, buttons, and stones as well as paper of different color and sizes is needed. I've learned from young people that remnants of felt, material, and ribbons can provide another dimension to the images they make.

In the following I talk about the process by referring to 'buttons.' In practice the child or young person knows he or she can, when making a picture, use a mixture of shells, buttons and stones, plus any other small craft items on the table.

When they show an interest in the buttons, I suggest how we could use them to help me understand who is who in their family. They will choose which buttons to use to represent the people they want to show. Pets also can be included. I explain that when the picture is finished I will take a photograph and then together we will put the buttons back into the button dish.

The act of returning the buttons to their dish is a way of grounding the child, of physically getting him or her to put the issues away and return to the everyday world. Ensure there is time for the child or young person to do something 'lighter' before the session ends.

When a young person decides he or she wants to work with the buttons I ask him or her to choose a piece of paper and a button that represents him or her. They can then go on to pick buttons for the people and pets they want to include.

Initially, the child or young person may randomly pick up buttons and place them without much thought but, as working with images draws on the right side of the brain which is non verbal, spatial, spontaneous, intuitive, creative, and non-judgmental (Sperry, 1973, quoted in Silverstone 1999, p. 4) young people become engrossed in creating and showing their world without thinking, analyzing, or judging, the mode of the left brain. At this stage simply observe without making any comments, noting, without interpreting, the child's process. Where interpretations are made it pollutes the image and is usually the therapist or helpers 'stuff.' Oaklander (1978) believes if the therapist has good will and is able to pull back from making an interpretation or judgment then there is no way a mistake can be made. She comments that while most of us have good will, very few of us are able to refrain from making judgments, or have awareness that we are interpreting the child's work. Silverstone, (1997) notes that the person who does not interpret knows best.

How the young people make a choice can give insight into their world. Observing from the moment a piece of paper is chosen through to how the child makes his or her button choices is, therefore, important, noticing:

- How the child makes his or her choices, thoughtfully, quickly.
- The order in which buttons are chosen.
- Where buttons are placed.
- Where the position of a button is changed or a button is removed from the paper.
- How different buttons are handled and touched.

Non-judgmental, non-interpretative facilitation of the work is vital.

****

WORKING WITH BUTTONS – JOE

Joe's father had died by suicide suicide eighteen months before he came to see me, when Joe was eleven. Now in secondary school, he was having problems managing his anger, at school and at home. Although I knew how Joe's father had died, I stayed with his reason for coming– 'I hate being angry all the time.'

Joe was quiet, withdrawn and found eye contact awkward. As many young people find talking face-to-face with an adult difficult I find a distraction helps. Squashy balls, bean bags, malleable objects give young people something to 'do' with their hands that helps unlock their tongues and it was while Joe was making shapes with play dough and then touching and making patterns with the buttons, that he began to tell me something of his immediate world, how he loved football, especially being goalie.

I tentatively asked if his dad had liked football. No verbal response but his body language was 'don't go there.' I felt I'd asked about his father too soon. I reflected to Joe that I could see he didn't want to talk about his dad and that was okay. I sat for a few seconds thinking I'd been clumsy when Joe asked if I knew about football. I told him, "The basics, yes, but I'd never understood the 'off-side' rule."

Joe decided to teach me. Using the buttons, he set up scenarios to demonstrate when a player was 'off-side.' This session marked a change; our relationship seemed more secure and Joe felt he could be himself, as happened in the following weeks when he came in and used the buttons to set up football games. Throughout he never mentioned his father or talked about his anger.

When I sensed Joe was ready, I asked if we could do something different with the buttons: ' look at who was who in his family.' I explained how we would do this and he agreed. Initially he quickly put any buttons down but then his pace slowed and he became more thoughtful not only about the buttons he selected but where he placed them.

Below is Joe's first button picture.

Joe's first image

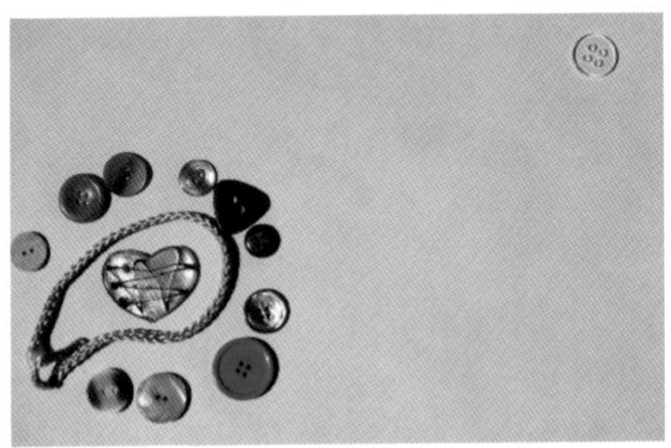

The button Joe chose to represent himself is in the top right-hand corner.

I began by pointing to this button,

'Tell me about this button, Joe?"

"I wanted that button because it's big but sort of invisible, like me." Joe then spoke about each button, who it was, his reasons for choosing that particular button. We looked at size, color, and placing and where appropriate I'd ask,

"Is that telling you anything, Joe?" To begin Joe would just shrug, but as he became immersed in his image he made his own links and was able to talk about his family.

I was aware Joe hadn't once mentioned the large heart-shaped button and what he had placed around it. Although I knew Joe's dad had hung himself I didn't want to assume Joe had placed this there as a representation of a rope. I pointed to the heart-shaped button,

"And this button, Joe?"

No reply and then, very quietly, "Dad."

He offered no more so I reflected on what I was seeing.

"This is your dad and," circling the braid with my finger, "this part?"

"What he did?"

He offered no more so I simply reflected what he had said. "This is your dad and what he did and around him you've placed your family and friends, but I'm also noticing where you've put yourself."

The words exploded from Joe.

"Nobody tells me anything, I know they're talking about Dad, but they shut up when they see me. I want to know stuff, but they don't tell me. They think I'm still a kid."

Joe then touched his 'dad' and began talking about why he'd chosen that button. The blue in the button was the color of their football team. The black, his dad's hands when he'd been repairing cars while the underneath of the button, a dark grey, was depression.

When I felt he was ready, I asked Joe if he could use the buttons to show any changes he would like to make. He first put his dad's button next to his own, but then returned it to its original position. Joe then placed the buttons as shown below.

Joe's second image

Here Joe has put himself in the centre of his family and also closer to the reality of his father's suicide.

As we explored the second image Joe was able to express his need to feel included, to understand more of what had happened.

When ending a 'button' session, have the young person help you put the buttons back into the container. This practical task is a way of grounding and returning the young person to the here and now as he or she physically puts away and leaves behind difficult feelings and issues.

Where a button has been used to represent the person who has died, I ask if they want to keep that button. If "Yes," I suggest we do something special with 'dad's button,' perhaps carefully wrapping it in tissue paper and placing it safely in the box. This can help with accepting the loss and saying goodbye.

Art

While for some young people 'the doing' is the therapy with no need for words, for others, their image brings into the 'here and now' feelings and concerns that 'talking' would take longer to access.

On the Hoof

Often, artwork with young people is 'on the hoof'– they seem comfortable with spontaneously creating images. As I have said for some 'the doing' is the therapy while for others exploring their image enables them to share feelings and concerns they would not otherwise talk about.

Sometimes there is a need to give reassurance to those who say 'but I can't draw!' It's not about technique! For those who insist they 'can't draw' yet there is a sense they would like to, Oaklander's (1988) 'scribble pictures' are a way of overcoming the 'can't draw belief'.

When a young person is trying to tell me about a strong emotion or an incident, where appropriate, I ask them if they could paint or draw it.

Leah, an eleven-year-old girl, was having dreams about a one eyed monster. Understandably, this frightened her. I asked if she wanted to show me the monster in a picture. Using a lead pencil she drew a very small monster that could hardly be seen then quickly tore it up. Even when contained on paper, this monster was still too frightening for Leah.

The following week she asked if she could make another picture. This time although still faint the monster had grown in size and Leah told me that not only did she dream about it but thought it was in her house.

Leah's second picture

When we next met Leah spoke almost immediately of the monster being in her house. I asked if she could draw her house and show me where the monster was in her house.

Leah's Monster in the House

The picture she drew focused on one room. Although there is color in the picture, again the monster is in pencil, lying in a chair. Leah began to talk about the girl who lived in the house. How early one morning the girl had gone downstairs and found the monster with its one eye wide open, lying in the chair. The girl knew the monster was dead but couldn't understand why it was smiling.

And then Leah moved from the third to the first person and began telling me how early one morning she had found her dad. She knew he was dead but couldn't understand why he was smiling.

" My dad never smiled, he was always sad." (Leah's dad had severe clinical depression.)

One of her dad's eyes had been wide open, the other closed. Leah hadn't known what to do so had gone back to her room. She'd not told anyone about her experience.

Leah's image was a turning point and over several months she was able to share her confusion and difficult feelings, as well as talk about her father, his depression, and her experience of finding his body.

She was able to talk of how she'd heard the word 'suicide' and now, knowing what it meant, her fear, that her mum, who also had depression, might do the same thing.

Children do not know how to grieve and the different feelings they experience can be confusing and wrongly labeled. Images, activities in whatever form can, says Oaklander (2006), give children a safe distance from which to explore their experiences and, with the help of the therapist, be gently supported to acknowledge and own their feelings. In doing so the young person can begin to move through the grief process.

Art also provides a route through which fears and everyday concerns, both realistic and unrealistic, can be seen and gently worked through enabling the child to have a clearer narrative of what has been a traumatic event in their life.

In this chapter there has only been space to share a few examples of how working creatively can help young people. Malchiodi (2003) comments on the powerful tool that art is in visually communicating thoughts and feelings that are too painful to voice, to give words to. It is vital, therefore, that anyone wanting to work in this field has appropriate training. For those wishing to know more about art facilitation skills, The Person Centered Art Therapy Association in the UK offers training in Person Centered Art therapy skills at both certificate and diploma level.

To protect confidentiality, all names have been changed.

References

Gross, J., & Haynes, H. (1998). Drawing facilitates children's verbal reports of emotionally laden events. *Journal of Experimental Psychology*, 4, 163-179.

Hall, E., Hall, C. A., & Stradling, P. (2006). *Guided imagery*. London: Sage.

Malchiodi, C. A. (2003). *Handbook of art therapy*. New York: Guilford Press.

Mearns, D. (2005). *Working at a relational depth in counseling & psychotherapy*. London: Sage.

Oaklander, V. (1978). *Windows to our children*. New York: The Gestalt Journal Press.

Oaklander, V. (2006). *Hidden treasure: A map to the child's inner self*. London: Karnac Books.

Rogers, C. R. (1961). *A way of being*. New York: Rutledge.

Rogers, E. (2007). *The art of grief*. New York: Rutledge.

Silverstone, L. (1999). *Art therapy: The person centred way*. London: Jessica Kingsley.

Sperry, R. W. (1973) Lateral specialization of cerebral function in the surgically separated hemispheres. In B. McGuigan & R. A. Schoonover (Eds.), *Psychophysiology of thinking* (pp. 5-19). New York: Academic Press.

****

DIDI HIRSCH MENTAL HEALTH SERVICES AND THE SURVIVOR MOVEMENT

By Rick Mogil
Didi Hirsh Mental Health Services

Most of what we know about the beginnings of the survivor program at Didi Hirsch Mental Health Services in Los Angeles, California, one of the first programs developed for survivors of suicide, comes from interviews with and the writings of Norman Farberow, Ph.D. (co-founder of the first suicide prevention center and crisis line in the United States); Mickey Heilig, LCSW; former Executive Director of the Suicide Prevention Center, Janet Belland Galea; and survivor Lois Bloom.

It would be specious of me to state that the premier United States suicide prevention crisis line also provided the first survivor groups. According to the information in a booklet published by the collaborative efforts of the World Health Organization and the International Association for Suicide Prevention, "self-help support groups became popular after the Second World War" with suicide bereavement groups beginning in the 1970s (WHO/IASP, 2008, p. 3). Dr. Farberow wrote in *Surviving Suicide* that the process of a "psychological autopsy" provided researchers "first hand awareness of the reactions of the survivors" (2008 p, 6). Survivor bereavement has its own set of complications involving stigma and taboo. The Suicide Prevention Center founders, realizing the extent of the effect of loss on survivors, attempted to provide groups to facilitate bereavement therapy in the 1970s.

The lack of participation in those early groups was attributed to the fact that survivors were not looking for therapy, rather a safe place to talk about what they were feeling and seeking "non-judgmental emotional support" with others who had experienced a loss to suicide (Farberow,

2008, p. 6). It was not long after this period that a young woman, Janet Belland, came to the Suicide Prevention Center to volunteer for the crisis line.

Janet has been described as "a gentle, compassionate, soft spoken woman" (Bloom, 2009, p. 5). She was determined to complete the training, but during one of the role-play sessions, she had decided to role play her brother who had died by suicide a year earlier. Janet talked to me about the emotional tsunami that swept over her during the session and how Mickey Heilig, then Executive Director of the Suicide Prevention Center, took her aside, comforted her, and asked, "Why are you here?" Janet told Mickey the story of her loss and how she wanted to help others like her brother. But more importantly, she wanted to talk to others like herself, other survivors.

Janet's desire fell in line with the Suicide Prevention Center founders' belief that survivors were an important component of their work. Their interviews with Janet led to the questions that plagued survivors (it needs to be stated that many of the answers survivors seek are never uncovered and the best we can hope for is acceptance of this and a willingness to move forward) and they set Janet and Mickey to the task of developing a survivor program.

Janet and Mickey discussed group dynamics, how long should each meeting last, how many sessions should each group meet, optimum number of participants, and topics of discussion. They decided that eight weeks of one-and-a-half hour meetings would suffice. When asked why an eight-week group and not a nine or ten, Janet replied, "We wanted the group long enough for participants to bond and short enough that it wouldn't feel like a lifetime." She also felt that the group should be mixed as to relationships to their loved ones, comprised of various losses: child, parent, sibling, spouse, co-worker, friend, and others.

I asked Dr. Farberow, in a recent discussion, about the reasons for the mixed group. He related that it would provide individuals perspectives they might not have considered. For example, parents might hear what children feel about the loss of their parent, or hear how the loss might have affected their other children and children might discover how a child's suicide could affect the family.

Everyone involved agreed that a peer lead group with a licensed therapist facilitator was the key to the group success. Survivor co-facilitators provide new members hope for a future beyond their loss while therapists provide stability.

Janet and Mickey developed agendas as guidelines for each week and collected material (articles, quotes, excerpts from leading journals, books, and other published works) for survivors to read at their leisure.

Janet had been working in the entertainment field for years and was instrumental in the Suicide Prevention Center obtaining a grant from the Entertainment Industry Foundation to fund the survivor program. Her connections also allowed her to garner television interviews for her, Mickey, and other survivors to talk about the program and invite viewers to join them. The first group began in late 1981.

Dr. Farberow wrote, "Mickey Heilig and Janet Belland developed a program which, with very few modifications, has proved over the years to be both effective and gratifying." He also said, "The survivor movement in the United States was initiated primarily by survivors who looked for help from the mental health professionals but didn't find it" (2008, p. 6).

The development of the Survivors After Suicide program at Didi Hirsch Mental Health Services would not be complete without the story of Lois and Sam Bloom though. Shortly after the suicide of their son, Sammy, in 1982, Lois and Sam were encouraged to call the Los Angeles Suicide Prevention Center for group information. Lois wrote about that first encounter saying, "I desperately needed help. After talking to Janet, I felt if anyone could help me, it was she" (Bloom, 2009, p. 5).

Janet, Mickey, and the Survivors After Suicide program brought more than just "help" to Lois and Sam. They received training to become co-facilitators, established the first Survivors After Suicide newsletter (Lois was the first editor) and, with their new-found hope, were instrumental in establishing SPAN-California (Suicide Prevention Advocacy Network), an organization that promotes stopping suicide through awareness at the grassroots level and advocating for suicide prevention through legislation. They both have spent countless hours before local, state, and federal agencies supporting suicide prevention and survivor programs, were awarded the "Survivor(s) of the Year" award in 1998 by the American Association of Suicidology, and currently serve on the Survivors After Suicide advisory board at Didi Hirsch.

In 1988, the Suicide Prevention Center was struggling to remain solvent. Sources of funding had been dwindling and executive staff was forced to seek support from other agencies. Family Services of Los Angeles (FSLA) brought the Suicide Prevention Center and its Survivors After Suicide program, within their purview until 1997 when Didi Hirsch Mental Health Services rescued the then-failing FSLA.

The Survivors After Suicide program has remained unchanged over the past twenty-nine years and has been supported through the generous donations of the survivors and grants from private and public sources. Funds have recently become available through Proposition 63, the Mental Health Services Act in California, to expand the Survivors After Suicide program in Los Angeles County and to bring survivor services to our neighbors in Orange County.

Where do we go from here? The next step in our growth is to bring monolingual groups in Spanish, Korean, Vietnamese, Farsi, and Arabic to our programs as these are the leading minority languages in Los Angeles and Orange counties after English.This will be accomplished through partnerships with agencies serving these communities.

When I became a survivor in 2003, through the suicide of my younger brother Ed (another story for another time), I was devastated and alone. I was given a referral to Didi Hirsch's Survivors After Suicide program and found a safe haven to talk about my fears, desolation, anger, and guilt. I began to think that we could end suicide by educating the public, ending the stigma and breaking the taboos. Realistically, we can reduce the number of suicides per year or the rate of suicide per 100,000 population. But there always will be survivors and there always will be members of our community who will, with compassion, dedication, and love, provide services and groups for those bereaved by suicide.

References

Bloom, L. (2009, July/August/September). Our summer potluck – A time to share. *Survivors After Suicide Newsletter*, *22*(2), p. 5.

Farberow, N. (2008, Fall). Norm Farberow shares his recollections of the history of the survivor movement. *Surviving Suicide*, *20*(3), pp. 5-6.

World Health Organization & International Association for Suicide Prevention. (2008). Preventing suicide: How to start a survivors' group. Geneva: Department of Mental Health and Substance Abuse, World Health Organization. Retrieved August 25, 2010 at *www.who.int/mental_health/prevention/suicide/resource_survivors.pdf*

****

HOW PETS COMFORT PEOPLE DURING GRIEF

By Michelle Linn-Gust, Ph.D.

In the United States, people are more likely to have a dog as a pet than any other animal and the number of pets in households is growing. According to the American Pet Product Manufacturers Association (APPMA) 2009-10 survey, 71.4 million homes in the United States have a pet (it was 62 million in 2008) and of those, 45.6 million have a dog. Cats trail second, living in 38.2 million homes, and freshwater fish are a distant third in 13.3 million homes. Many other countries have similar increases relating to pets.

As the number of pets grows in homes, so does the amount of money people spend on them. The APPMA estimated that in 2010 people would spend 47.7 billion US dollars on their pets. This number has continued to grow over the years as the aisles in large chain stores grow with pet-related supplies, pet stores expand, and web sites offer easy ordering for products. People are spending more money on food (and being more aware of what ingredients go into the food they buy for their pets), more money on veterinarian visits (thus also extending the lives of their pets), and on ancillary items like clothing, leashes, and toys.

Dogs are now more likely than in the past to have their own beds in their homes (sometimes these beds are elevated off the ground) rather than sleeping outside in the yard or in a doghouse. They also might travel with their families on vacation (thus the number of hotels that accept pets has increased) and have their own health insurance. Cats have similar luxuries.

As people spend more money on their pets and more time with them, they also are more likely to consider them members of the family. In the face of the changing family in today's society (an increase in single-sex, two-couple homes; people living further from family; people waiting longer to marry if they marry at all), a pet can sometimes serve as another family member or the pet can be a person's only family member.

Pets are important in grief because sometimes they provide support people don't believe they get from other sources and they also might be the last connection to the person who died. Pets sometimes are a basic way for people to stay connected to life. When people feel like their worlds have ended, they are filled with emotions and confused about why a loved one has ended his or her life, but a pet still needs to be fed, walked, and have playtime.

Obviously the needs of animals vary by the species as dogs can be more work than a cat. Dogs usually are walked and are more social creatures than cats. But what they provide for the humans is usually in line with the human's lifestyle (which also sometimes dictates which type of pet they have if they only have one although the number of homes is increasing with multiple numbers and types of pets).

For dogs who are used to being walked each day, those walks can be the social connection for grieving people who might otherwise not be socially engaged because of their sadness over the loss, particularly suicide loss because of the stigma. People are more likely to have a conversation with another human when walking a dog than without one and walking a dog also is a way to keep people active (Beck, 1999).

One major function that most species provide (at least the furry ones) is giving people a companion to pet and sit and listen to them tell the story of what happened to the loved one. Particularly after a suicide death, the bereaved are looking for someone to listen to them tell the loved one's story repeatedly because in telling the story, one often finds a release and can reframe what happened to the loved one. They might not believe, again because of the stigma, that many people will listen. For some people after the death of a loved one, having the pet there, who doesn't talk back or judge them for what they feel, gives them support they do not believe they are not getting from their human loved ones.

Having a pet in the house for many people decreases their loneliness because the house does not feel as empty after the loved one dies, especially when that loved one was the only other human in the house. There still is the sound of a pet's nails walking across a wood floor or the jingling of the pet's tags when it moves.

Some people appreciate the funny antics of a pet in a time where it does not feel like there is much laughter. The pet continues to chase a ball or jump over the couch when it's not supposed to. Laughter often is a way to help one heal and feel something other than sadness during grief. It is a way of reminding grieving people they are still alive and can feel good.

Most of what pets provide for people is comfort in non-verbal ways. While people sometimes talk to their pets, the pets usually are not talking back (at least not in English!). What people receive from their pets can be as simple as being in a room together and not interacting in any verbal way.

However, what is interesting about pets and families is that pets do not contribute to a family's income (Albert & Bulcroft, 1988), but instead provide people with other kinds of support. While the pet can't speak and say exactly what it is giving the human (or getting from the human) seeing a wagging tail at the front door lets them think the dog is happy, too.

Ultimately, what pets provide is a focus for people after a human loved one has died. Grief is a confusing process, but having the stability of knowing a pet is there and needs its day-to-day needs met (like being fed) is part of a routine that is often left out as an important part of coping with grief. Life is about routine and while often it has changed when someone loved has died, the needs of the pet haven't and that forces people to be cognizant in ways they might not be otherwise because they are caught up in the sadness of their loss.

In a society where pets often are considered family members, people use them in a myriad of ways after the death of a human loved one. And as each person will travel a slightly different grief road, the type of pet needed and the companionship sought will be different. Pets can be a source of strength for people in a time when they don't realize they have any strength or any love to give. And what they receive back from the pet, although not measurable in any true human scale, is priceless.

References

Albert, A., & Bultcroft, K. (1988). Pets, families, and the life course. *Journal of Marriage and the Family,* 50, 543-552.

American Pet Products Manufacturers Association (2010). Industry statistics & trends. Retrieved July 9, 2010, from *www.appma.org/press_industrytrends.asp?Printlt=1.*

****

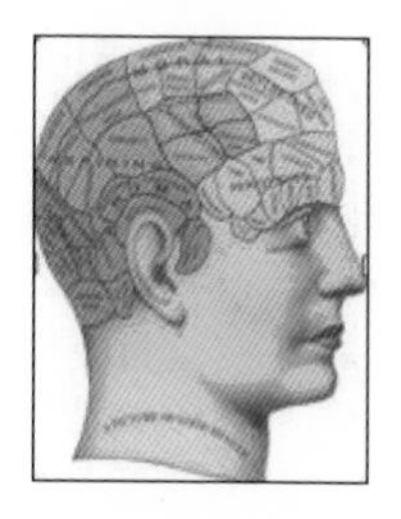

A MENTAL HEALTH WORKER'S EXPERIENCES OF A PATIENT'S SUICIDE: JOHN

By Mark Haith, MA

Introduction

This chapter addresses the impact made by the suicide of a patient upon me as a mental health nurse and tutor. Patient suicide is an aspect of mental health nursing experienced by a significant number of mental health workers at some point during their career (Valente & Saunders, 2002). Staff fears of potential patient suicide is influential on the practices undertaken within mental health nursing, and is recognized as a major source of stress in the profession (Gaffney et al., 2009). Consequently, an important means of preventing "burn out" and maintaining effective working in health and social care work is through the processes of supervision and self-reflection (Ghaye, 2005). This chapter therefore aims to be useful both for the author in his own process of self-development, and also in supporting other members of the caring professions who have experienced the suicide of one of their patients.

In writing this account I have been surprised by the emotional demands and awkwardness of knowing how to proceed. As a result I sought the structure offered by the model of reflection described by Taylor (2000). This is a three stage process, which asks the user to describe the events that have occurred, examine interpretations that can be applied to these events, and identify what has been learnt from undertaking this reflective process. I have used this approach to reflect on my experience of a patient's suicide for the purpose of developing my future practice as a mental health worker and teacher (Taylor, 2000; Ghaye, 2005). The names of the patient and staff members described in this account have been changed to ensure their confidentiality is respected. Furthermore, some of the details of events are kept vague in order to keep the patients' identity private.

The account I am describing occurred some years ago. At the time I was working as a mental health-nursing assistant in a psychiatric unit for adults. I had been in post for around a year and was spending a lot of time working directly with the unit's service users. One of the patients I had spent a lot of time working with was John.

Shortly before John's suicide I took two weeks holiday from work. When I returned I was surprised by a change in John's behavior and mood. He seemed very small physically and emotionally, acting in a manner I was unfamiliar with from my previous encounters with him. I was surprised John was not his usual expressive self. I asked another member of staff what was going on for John and she told me that he was going out a lot and was getting ready to move on from the hospital. I thought this change in behavior was strange and I felt uneasy, but not particularly alarmed by it. It is usual on a psychiatric ward to see a patient's moods fluctuate on a regular basis, something I accepted as far from unusual. I found out later that John had been visiting people he used to know and had been to look at the place where he was to kill himself.

When I came onto the ward for my shift the next afternoon I was told that something serious had happened, and was surprised that John had attempted to kill himself but was alive in hospital. I wonder if the other staff were holding back the seriousness of his injuries or it was my way of dealing with this news because I assumed that he was going to make a full recovery given time. I remember the ward was very quiet and calm during the afternoon, during which news came that John had died. This was his third attempt to kill himself, so recognizing that he wanted to die was very important for me at this time. I felt sad but calm (rather than strongly emotional) when we received the news that he had died soon after arriving in hospital.

The ward manager informed the team that as a legal requirement John would have to be identified. I asked if it would help if I accompanied whoever did it. He replied, "No, as it would have to be a senior manager's job." However, on finishing his shift he asked me if I could undertake this task, having left the details of where to go on his desk. The staff nurse in charge seemed shocked by the way this matter was handled and told me I did not have to do it because it was not part of my role as a nursing assistant. I felt a responsibility to be involved in the process so, despite feeling disappointed as how it was handled, I accepted the task. Although some co-workers verbalized concerns for my wellbeing, no one took up my offer to come with me. The task of accompaniment and support I had offered to undertake had changed to one of sole responsibility for identification without consultation with me. I remain cynical as to the genuineness of this concern as no one acted directly to support me in identifying John's body. I remember finding the attitude of other staff members irritating in the following few days as they seemed to avoid involvement in what I saw as the very important duty of undertaking processes required following our patient's death. John was a person we knew and he was someone's son, so I felt as a mental health unit we had a duty to do our best for him. I saw this as a vital part of our job and I was not prepared to avoid my responsibilities even if my more experienced colleagues were doing so. On reflection the anger I felt then is gone but I remain disappointed that senior staff chose to expose me as a very junior staff member to this emotionally challenging leadership role.

The possibility that it might be appropriate to feel sad occurred to me suddenly when I met the hospital staff who had been trying to save John's life. I was surprised to find the surgical sister (nurse) had tears in her eyes when we talked about what had happened to John. I remember telling her that John was a good person, he was intelligent and kind to other people. She seemed quite upset by this, I guess because it added human depth to the unconscious body she had been working to prevent dying. When she took me to see John I was surprised to see what he looked like. I knew he had fallen from a cliff so expected to see him severely injured and bloody. There were no visible wounds or blood and he did not look dead to me. I laughed at his nose, which had been pushed back and widened. It really looked like a pig's snout and I could hear John's voice in my head moaning about messing his face up. I felt accepted by the sister for my reaction as perfectly appropriate. This was very supportive. I also met the surgeon who had operated on John, he and the sister allowed me to ask as many questions as I needed to about John's death. This attitude was very different to that of my own unit where discussion seemed to be feared and avoided.

I was asked by our ward manager to attend the coroner's court. I was not sure what I had to do in this role and on reflection I don't think the other staff knew either. Fear of going to court is a common theme in mental health nursing. I became nervous when I was asked to swear on the Bible but the officials were very supportive and only asked me if the body I identified was John's. I assumed the ward manager was scared about being cross examined about failing to prevent this patient's death so was actively avoiding going to court. Because I did not raise this topic with him I am not sure if this was actually the case. I am glad I went because I heard witness statements about John's death that other ward staff missed. I particularly recall a witness who had seen John prior to jumping from the cliff– he had acknowledged her and had smiled. I was disappointed that our unit did not seek to support these witnesses considering what they had seen occur. I was annoyed that no one on the ward asked me what had happened at court or how I felt about it when I could have benefitted from their support.

My final involvement with John involved going to his funeral service, which was held at the hospital. I was very angry on that day, mainly concerning my view of the hospital's competence in preventing his death. On reflection I do not see this as a useful expression of energy; instead I try and make positive use of events by highlighting the changes in his presentation as a warning sign when discussing suicide risk with students.

I think John's death shocked other staff more than I realized at the time. I was angry with what I saw as our ward manager's attempts to avoid speaking to John's mother at his funeral service. I can understand the potential for emotional distress in such a situation but I believe this woman was owed the respect of a prompt face-to-face meeting. The ward seemed to function as normal for a while but I think it is no coincidence that a number of senior staff left the unit over the next few months. I believe patient suicides are events that can potentially make or break a mental health team. If staff is able to "emotional download" and practical initiatives preventing further avoidable suicides do not occur, the ability of the team to work together may be compromised.

I found working with John interesting, funny and moving. Although I did my best to maintain professional boundaries there were clearly elements of friendship between John and I. This level of engagement with John possibly accounts for my feeling overly distant from many of my clients since. There seems a fine line between being emotionally open when working with service users without feeling emotionally vulnerable. I feel pushed into an emotional middle ground where I will not be too affected if a patient kills him or herself. I wish rather to value the emotional experience of working closely with clients as it occurs, to accept a client has the right to choose to kill oneself, but equally to remember the client's responsibility for his or her own actions. With John, this meant my accepting the reality of his life and his long-term felt need to take control by ending living. On several occasions John had discussed "doing what I want to do with my life." At the time I thought he was referring to returning to university. I now believe he was discussing his desire to kill himself.

Reflective analysis

Having described events as they occurred to me, there follows a reflective summary of events, interpretations, and personal learning undertaken using Taylors' model of reflection (2000).

What occurred?	What interpretation can be applied to events?	What have I learnt?
Subduing of John's behaviour and mood	Changes in John's mood from his usual observed patterns may suggest he had made a clear decision to kill himself	The importance of the warning signs of potential increased suicide risk which I can inform students about
I assumed John was injured but would survive his suicide attempt	Staff were concealing the seriousness of John's injuries; staff were not fully informed themselves of the severity; I interpreted things as I wished to see them	Some questions can not be answered but it is normal and acceptable for this to occur
I identified John's body despite it seeming to be an inappropriate role for a junior member of staff	The ward manager could have taken personal responsibility or assigned another member of staff to undertake this role; other people recognised my emotional strengths and willingness to undertake the task	I put myself through a difficult process for the sake of others I acted as a leader in a situation where others were too scared to do so Being angry about other people's faults is not productive

I experienced acceptance, patience and kindness from the surgical staff who had tried to save John's life	They seemed to genuinely care about the welfare of John and myself and had a positive emotional experience from learning something about John from me	It is possible to work in a stressful aspect of healthcare and remain emotionally open to patients and other staff undergoing traumatic events, even if my experience of working in mental health teams in this sense has been mixed
Lack of support from my direct colleagues when attending coroners court, but support from staff there	The ward manager was scared to attend, and other staff avoided going with me despite suggesting they were there to support me Staff outside of the mental health system may be more capable of expressing concern for others	I learnt a lot about how the court runs which is important for my teaching and practice I had invaluable further insight into John's death which answered some questions for me and helped me resolve feelings about the situation
Lack of support from ward staff for their own staff, witnesses, and family members affected by John's death	Staff fear of being blamed for inadequacy of action in regards to John's death Fear of discussing difficult issues due to levels of emotion involved The impact of John's suicide on the dissolution of the team over following months	This has illustrated to me a clear need for structured support for all involved in the suicide of a patient for their immediate and long-term emotional health The need for structured ongoing measures to prevent avoidable suicides and staff burnout
Developing an emotionally open relationship with John	John's suicide has impacted on my ability to engage emotionally with clients	Recognizing the need to appreciate the lessons learned from working with John but not to assume similarities with all other clients

Writing this reflective piece	New memories and questions about what happened have emerged as a consequence of writing this piece.	This open style of writing is more difficult than I assumed I feel I have done myself and John a service by writing about it and hope it is of some benefit to readers

Conclusion

John's suicide has been a highly influential event in my mental health teaching and practice. It has led me to be wary of emotional attachment to patients. It also has made me keen to use the opportunities I have to make a difference and reminds me why I became a mental health nurse in the first place. I maintain my belief formed at the time that John achieved what he wanted by killing himself, even though I wish he had not done so. I accept that this was his decision to make, not mine. Some of the questions those left behind ask when people kill themselves were answered for me through talking to other staff about what they knew about what happened, listening to witness statements, and recalling my conversations with John prior to his death. Moving from not knowing to partially knowing has helped me appreciate more the position of friends and relatives in their search for answers about what happened and why when they are left behind. The impact of a patients' suicide on individual staff and mental health teams is not to be overlooked.

References

Gaffney, P., Russell, V., Collins, K., Bergin, A., Halligan, P., Carey, C., & Coyle, S. (2009). Impact of patient suicide on front-line staff in Ireland. *Death Studies*, 33, 639-656.

Ghaye, T. (2005). *Developing the Reflective Healthcare Team.* Oxford: Blackwell.

Taylor, B. (2000). *Reflective practice: A guide for nurses and midwives.* Buckingham: Open University Press.

Valente, S., & Saunders, J. (2002). Nurses' grief reactions to a patient's suicide *Perspectives in Psychiatric Care,* 38(1), 5-14.

****

SO HOW EXACTLY DO I HELP SOMEONE WHO IS BEREAVED?

By Michelle Linn-Gust, Ph.D.

Editor's Note: Adapted from "Notes for Caregivers, Clinicians, Friends, and Other Supports" in *Rocky Roads: The Journeys of Families through Suicide Grief* by Michelle Linn-Gust, Chellehead Works, Albuquerque, NM, 2010.

If you want to help someone you care about who is bereaved by suicide, your first concern is to examine your own view of death and then your view of suicide. You must understand your own attitudes and beliefs before you can help other people.

As a 21-year-old when my sister died, I had a hard time understanding that some people in my life reacted as they did because of their own experiences with suicide. It took me about ten years to fully comprehend this idea, and it happened by means of a friendship with someone I worked with at the *Ball State Daily News*. Although I knew his family had not been healthy, I did not remember that he had shared long before Denise died that his father had been suicidal at various times, often putting the family in harm's way. When Denise died and he backed away from me, it was sad to me because he was someone I worked with every day and considered a good friend. Our friendship was never the same although we worked together for about six more months. It ultimately severed a friendship and led to me leaving the newspaper during my senior year.

If you have experience with suicide in your past, please do not be afraid of the person you care about who is walking a grief journey. Share your story with them (or with someone else if you are not that comfortable) and let them know you have not abandoned them. They will appreciate your honesty and the opportunity to travel with you as you maneuver through your own life experience.

Not only should you be aware of your own experiences with death and suicide, but you also should understand the positive and negative emotions you have around them. Where do they come from? Why do you feel that way? Once you have spent time exploring them, you then can move on to helping others. It is imperative never to allow your own emotions to block how you help someone. This is particularly true for the suicide bereaved who already might have encountered a therapist/clinician/loved one who is uncomfortable with the topic and made it very clear to the bereaved. This validates the shame and stigma that the bereaved person is trying to overcome. Instead, be open to what the bereaved need you to hear. They might not know exactly how they need help but in listening to them, you can piece it together and help them understand where they are on the healing journey and where they need to go.

For the family that has lost someone to suicide, acknowledgment from the community is extremely important to their healing. While it is not expected that people will come and smother the family with casseroles (there really are only so many casseroles families can eat— think about how welcome a pizza might be one night!), it does help when people hear from their neighbors, and all the communities involved in their lives (work, school, neighborhood, church, and so forth). These communities are where we do most of our routine functioning, and to know that the community cares, is aware of what has happened and that it is devastating to the family, helps particularly after suicide because of the shame and stigma surrounding it.

Different people will offer help to each person who is grieving. Some people will have extended family members who come to help. Other people might live far away from extended families and instead may get help from neighbors. While the families appreciate any help they get after the loss, most of all they appreciate the acknowledgment of the loss.

The Internet has changed the way we grieve. People have places where they can reach out as never before. It is not just about status reports on Facebook that indicate someone has died, but there also are opportunities to talk about how much we miss the loved one and to share anniversaries as they approach. People want to know others are there for them and feeling their pain of the loss.

Because of the stress when someone dies, people often need to be guided and shown what to do. Families need one person to take a leadership role and manage everything, down to making sure that dinner gets on the table and the laundry is done. This does not need to happen forever, but it helps for at least the first few weeks to have some extra help. Or if one person can manage the people who want to offer more emotional and practical support, that is even better. The list of ways people can help is endless: bringing meals (those that can be frozen and then baked in the oven are very helpful; that way the family can access them as needed, especially on the bad days when dinner is almost impossible to get to the table); getting the children to and from school; answering phone calls and taking messages; cleaning the house/doing dishes/helping with the laundry; and anything else that might be important that the family is having a difficult time accomplishing.

I still have not forgotten the man who left a bag filled with paper plates, napkins, and plastic utensils on my family's doorstep after Denise died. I remember seeing him drive away and the card that he left. He said he did not know us but he felt like he needed to do something for us. And it helped not to have to worry about washing dishes for a few days. Often, the most appreciated gestures are so simple they do not even occur to us.

Sometimes the bereaved are not sure how to reach out for help. They might do it in what we consider strange or disconcerting ways like showing signs of suicidal ideation themselves. Don't be afraid to ask them if they are suicidal. When someone is suicidal, it is very difficult for people to reach out to the people in pain. People are afraid to ask. But by being afraid to ask, they are risking that person's life when what that person really wants is someone to throw a life preserver from the shore and let them know they can survive and make it back to land. If you ask, you really will not offend someone or put ideas into their heads, but you might save a life.

Be sure to have or be able to find some resources for someone who needs help. Even if you do not have them in hand, at least have an idea where to look on the Internet or in your local community. Keep in mind the needs of the individual you are trying to help, and that will be your guide to the resources that can best help them. The bereaved person also might have been frustrated by the lack of resources or may not be thinking clearly and having a difficult time finding the needed information. Therefore, your help will be even more appreciated.

Be sensitive to the cultural and religious backgrounds of the people you are trying to help. They might be family and you might be familiar with their backgrounds but those backgrounds also can be different from your own. And if you are working with people whose background is not familiar to you, take the time to understand their background. That will help you comprehend their views on suicide and death and make it easier for you to help them. The goal is not to change how or what a person believes but to help them process their views and find comfort in the loss of someone they cared about.

Beliefs are not the only difference that can make working with other cultural groups a challenge. Actions can vary as much as beliefs. For instance, it might be acceptable for a person from another culture to take long pauses while speaking. The silence might be important to them and part of the story as they are telling it. A helper could be ready to jump in and say something, whereas the bereaved person is not finished and might get frustrated with the helper. The helper should be patient and allow people to take their time when speaking. In other cultures, it might not be acceptable for people to hug (the opposite of cultures and regions where hugging is very normal and an encouraged part of loss).

Be aware that touching another person might not be accepted. Asking the person is the best way to find out about his or her beliefs because information from other sources might not always be reliable for that person's cultural group, especially if there are deviations (maybe the majority does not hug but this particular person does).

As someone who wants to help a bereaved person, you are to be commended for wanting to reach out and provide support. Many people are too afraid to do what you are doing. It does not take a lot to help someone; mostly what is important is to be there for them and ask what they need. They will tell you and be grateful for what you offer.

You have the honor of accompanying them on this journey. The rocky road is not always an easy one and sometimes we need help with it. The bereaved person may not always ask for help or even realize they need it. But listening to the bereaved, whether to the words they speak or their body language and actions, will give you some idea of how to guide them.

One of the aspects of the grief process that is important is finding meaning in the loss of someone we love, particularly after suicide. Sometimes it is through discussing the loss with someone else that we are able to find that meaning, to understand it, to figure out how it fits in our worlds. But we need guidance with the puzzle pieces; we need to look for the people who want to guide us on that path and help us put the pieces together.

Listeners pick up on clues, ideas, and other significant ideas that the bereaved might not hear in their own words. Listeners connect problems the person might be having that they are not able to put together themselves. Maybe they cannot piece together events that are related to the loss, yet someone who is listening can help them do that. New listeners are a new audience for the story.

Most of all, anyone who travels the grief journey with someone they care about is offering part of themselves that they probably did not realize they had to help the bereaved through what could be the most difficult experience in anyone's life.

****

FINAL ENCOURAGEMENT

We started this book by paying tribute to the life and work of Edwin Shneidman who can be said to have laid the foundations to the science of suicidology with postvention as one of its three pillars.

We have come a long way since that pioneering work with Norman Farberow and others whilst at the same time society has modified its attitude to suicide and to survivors. We must be grateful for that early work as well as the continuing efforts by those still working in that field.

However, we cannot be complacent, and we continue to urge those who can in any way help to improve the support available to those who have been bereaved by suicide.

We hope that the cooperation in this book of a variety of contributors from many diverse backgrounds illustrates our view that we must work together, pooling our talents and experience for the benefits of those who unfortunately find themselves in the position of being a survivor.

The co-authors of this book have both completed advanced study following the loss of loved one to suicide and we urge those carrying our research to involve survivors in their research. They will benefit from both the experiences and the passion that many survivors can contribute. We are both engaged in the practice of bereavement support and again we urge professionals and volunteers to work more closely for mutual benefit to enrich their knowledge and benefit from the experience that can be offered by survivors.

Sometimes professionals may be overawed by the thought of having to deal with those bereaved by suicide. Few will have had training in this specialised field. We hope that this book will give some encouragement to you to help a survivor and to recognise some of the particular needs that survivors may have.

It may be appropriate to close with the words of Shneidman, at the conclusion of his last book, *Comprehending Suicidology:*

"Regrettably, I believe that all the demographic studies...... all the bio-chemical work....through the elegant laboratory experiments,psychological and psychiatric papers are at their best background hum or music. They fail to address the necessary cause of suicide. For me the core data to elicit from a suicidal person (are the) two core questions of clinical suicidology:

'Where do you hurt?" and "How can I help you?'" (2001, p. 203).

Reference

Shneidman E. (2001). *Comprehending suicidology: Landmarks in 20th-century suicidology*. Washington, DC: American Psychological Association.

****

RESOURCES

U.S. and Worldwide Web Sites

The Internet has changed resources in ways we never could have imagined just a short time ago. The resources below are not comprehensive by any means. Instead, we have listed the major resources for the bereaved by suicide. The number of web sites has greatly increased over the years. It is easy to Google "bereaved by suicide or "suicide survivors" and get pages of links. We have included links below that we have found helpful and complete over the years. You also will find more links on all of these web sites. The first three listed offer comprehensive information for all facets of suicide (prevention, intervention, postvention). Further contact information is available on the sites.

American Association of Suicidology
www.suicidology.org

American Foundation for Suicide Prevention
www.afsp.org

International Association for Suicide Prevention
www.iasp.info

The Dougy Center for Grieving Children and Families
www.dougy.org

Suicide Information and Education Center
www.suicideinfo.ca

Suicide Prevention Resource Center
www.sprc.org

Internet Bereaved by Suicide Support Groups
The main web site is www.pos-ffos.com

To join POS (Parents of Suicides) or FFOS (Friends and Families of Suicides), the quickest way is to either email Karyl Chastain Beal (arlynsmom@bellsouth.net) and ask for an application, or to go to *http://health.groups.yahoo.com/group/parentsofsuicides/* to sign up for POS or to *http://health.groups.yahoo.com/group/ffofsuicides/* to sign up for FFOS.

Other Web Sites

www.siblingsurvivors.com
www.bereavedbysuicide.com
www.heartbeatsurvivorsaftersuicide.com

UK Web sites

Surivors of Bereavement by Suicide
(specialist support for those bereaved by suicide)
www.uk-sobs.org.uk

Child Bereavement Charity
www.careforthefamily.org.uk

Compassionate Friends
www.tcf.org.uk

Compassionate Friends (siblings)
www.tcfsiblingsupport.org.uk

Cruse Bereavement Care
www.cruse.org.uk

Inquest (advice on handling inquests)
www.inquest.gn.apc.org

National Association of Widows
www.nawidows.org.uk

Papyrus: prevention of young suicide
www.papyrus-uk-org

WAY foundation (Widows and Young)
www.wayfoundation.org.uk

Winston's Wish for bereaved children and families
www.winstonswish.org

BOOKS

For Adults

After Suicide: Help for the Bereaved by Sheila Clark (Hill of Content, 1995).

Coping with Suicide by Maggie Helen (Sheldon Books, 2001).

A Long-Shadowed Grief: Suicide and its Aftermath by Harold Ivan Smith (Cowley, 2006).

Leaving You: The Cultural Meaning of Suicide by Lisa Lieberman (Ivan R. Dee, 2003).

No Time to Say Goodbye: Surviving the Suicide of a Loved One by Carla Fine (Doubleday, 1997).

November of the Soul: The Enigma of Suicide by George Howe Colt (Scribner, 2006).

Overcoming Grief by Sue Morris (Robinson, 2008).

A Special Scar by Alison Wetheimer (Routledge, 2001).

Touched by Suicide: Hope and Healing After Loss by Michael F. Myers and Carla Fine (Gotham, 2006).

Why People Die by Suicide by Thomas Joiner (Harvard University Press, 2005).

For Children:

But I Didn't Say Goodbye: Helping Children and Families After a Suicide by Barbara Rubel (Griefwork Center, revised 2009).

Helping Children Cope with Loss by Rosemary Wells (Sheldon, 1988).

The Invisible String by Patricia Karst (DeVorss, 2000).

The Red Chocolate Elephants: For Children Bereaved by Suicide by Diana Sands (Kerridale, in press).

The Red Chocolate Elephants: Children Bereaved by Suicide DVD film directed by Diana Sands (Kerridale, 2010).

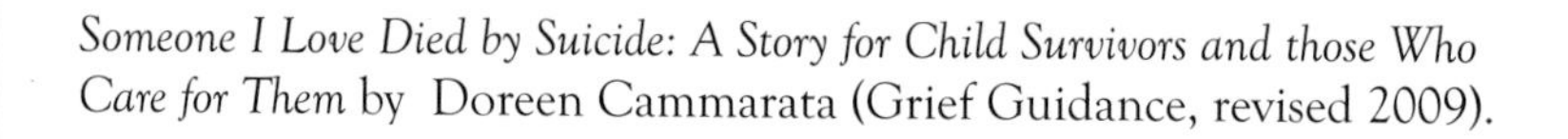

Someone I Love Died by Suicide: A Story for Child Survivors and those Who Care for Them by Doreen Cammarata (Grief Guidance, revised 2009).

<u>For Teens:</u>

After by Francis Chalifour (Tundra Books, 2005).

God and I Broke Up by Katarina Mazetti (Groundwood Books, 2005).